EMMA
THE TWICE-CROWNED
QUEEN

EMMA
THE TWICE-CROWNED
QUEEN
ENGLAND IN THE VIKING AGE

ISABELLA STRACHAN

PETER OWEN
LONDON AND CHESTER SPRINGS

PETER OWEN PUBLISHERS
73 Kenway Road, London SW5 0RE

Peter Owen books are distributed in the USA by
Dufour Editions Inc., Chester Springs, PA 19425-0007

First published in Great Britain 2004 by
Peter Owen Publishers

ISBN 0 7206 1221 7

Printed in Singapore by
Excel Print Media

To the memory of my mother, Florence,
and of my father, Andrew Wood, children's writer

ACKNOWLEDGEMENTS

My thanks are due to Southampton City Library, Archives and Information Services, and in particular the Reference Section, Southampton Central Library, and to the bookshops, especially Adrian Greenwood of Oxford and Patterson and Liddle of Bath, for providing me with the key volumes needed for this work; to the sources of the illustrations, in particular Westminster Abbey Library; also to Winchester Museums Service and Lincolnshire City and County Museum for giving me background details of the Saxon and Viking Ages and pointing me in the direction of further sources of information.

The cease of majesty

Dies not alone; but, like a gulf, doth draw

What's near with it: it is a massy wheel,

Fixed on the summit of the highest mount,

To whose huge spokes ten thousand lesser things

Are mortised and adjoined; which, when it falls,

Each small annexment, petty consequence,

Attends the boisterous ruin.

William Shakespeare, *Hamlet*, Act 3, Scene iii

Frailty, thy name is woman!

***Hamlet*, Act 1, Scene ii**

CONTENTS

VIKING SETTLEMENT AREAS IN BRITAIN

IRELAND AND NORTHERN FRANCE

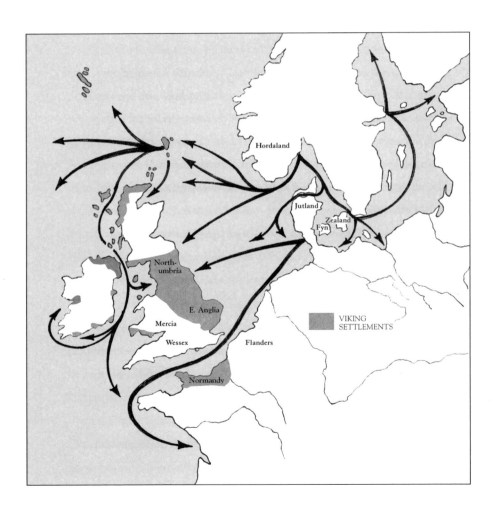

Hordaland

Jutland

Zealand

Fyn

North-
umbria

E. Anglia

Mercia

Wessex

Flanders

VIKING
SETTLEMENTS

Normandy

DRAMATIS PERSONAE

THE NORMANS AND FRENCH

Emma [known to the English as Elgiva, Aelfgifu, Aelfgyfu]
  (c. 984–1052): daughter of Richard, Duke of Normandy
  (d. 996) and Gunnor; queen first of Ethelred II then of
  Canute; mother of Edward the Confessor

Eustace (d. 1093): Count of Boulogne; son-in-law of Emma

Ralph (d. 1057): Earl of Hereford; grandson of Emma

Richard (d. 1026): Duke of Normandy; brother of Emma

Robert (d. 1035): Duke of Normandy; nephew of Emma

Robert of Jumièges (fl. 1043–55): Bishop of London; first
  Norman Archbishop of Canterbury

William (c. 1028–87): Duke of Normandy; William I of
  England, aka 'the Conqueror' and 'the Bastard'; son
  of Robert and Arlette [Herleva] and great-nephew of
  Emma

THE ENGLISH

Aldgyth (fl. 1016): wife of Ironside; cousin of Elgiva of Northampton

Aldgyth (fl. 1064–6): wife of Harold II

Alfred (c. 1013–36): second son of Emma and Ethelred;
  assassination procured by Harold I and Earl Godwin

Alphege [Aelfheah] (d. 1012): Archbishop of Canterbury; murdered by Danes at Greenwich

Edith [Eadgyth] (c. 1020–75): Edward the Confessor's queen; daughter of Godwin and Gytha

Edmund and **Edward** (c. 1016–57): sons of Ironside; brought up at the court of Stephen of Hungary (d. 1038)

Edmund Ironside (c. 993–1016): eldest surviving son of Ethelred's first marriage; attempted to hold England against Canute on Ethelred's death; briefly King of Wessex

Edric Streona (d. 1017): Earl of Mercia; son-in-law of Ethelred; blamed in *The Anglo-Saxon Chronicles* for the ultimate victory of the Danes

Edward the Confessor (c. 1003–66): King of England; eldest son of Emma and Ethelred; returned England to Saxon rule but wished to be succeeded by his Norman cousin, William; made a saint in 1161

Elfrida [Aelfthryth] (fl. 964–1000): King Edgar's queen; with Elfhere, Earl of Mercia, she engineered the assassination of Edward the Martyr at Corfe

Elgiva of Northampton [Aelfgifu] (fl. 1013–40): handfast wife of Canute; later Governor of Norway

Ethelred II the Unready [Aethelred] (c. 968–1016): King of England; son of Edgar and Elfrida; descendant of Alfred the Great; became king following the assassination of his half-brother, Edward the Martyr (c. 963–78); married Emma (second wife) to seal an alliance with Normandy against the Viking invasions of England

Goda [Godgifu] (*c.* 1007–1052): daughter of Emma and Ethelred; first husband Dreux [Drogo], Count of the Vexin (d. 1035); second husband Eustace of Boulogne

Godwin [Godwine] (d. 1053): Earl of Wessex; father-in-law of Edward the Confessor; father of Harold II; often misused his considerable power

Harold II (*c.* 1020–66): King of England; son of Godwin; slain at Hastings

Leofric (d. 1057): Earl of Mercia; husband of Lady Godiva [Godgifu] (d. 1067)

Stigand (*fl.* 1020–72): Emma's friend; Bishop of Winchester; Archbishop of Canterbury

Uhtred (d. 1016): Earl of Northumbria; son-in-law of Ethelred

Ulfcytel (d. 1016): Earl of East Anglia; son-in-law of Ethelred

Wulfstan (d. 1023): Archbishop of York

THE DANES

Canute [Cnut, Knutr] (*c.* 994–1035): King of England and Denmark; title of King of Norway disputed; second husband of Emma; ruler of short-lived North Sea Empire founded by his father

Estrid [Estrith] (*fl.* 1018): sister of Canute; with Earl Ulf ancestor of the medieval kings of Denmark

Gunhild [Gunnhild] (d. 1002): sister of Sweyn; killed in the St Brice's Day Massacre

Gunhild (*c.* 1021–38): daughter of Emma and Canute; married, under the name Kunigunde, Henry, King of Germany

Hardecanute [Harthacnut, Horthaknutr] (*c.* 1019–42): son of Emma and Canute; King of England; title of King of Denmark disputed

Harold I Harefoot (d. 1040): son of Canute and Elgiva, title of King of England disputed

Siward (d. 1055): Earl of Northumbria

Sweyn (d. 1036): son of Canute and Elgiva, Governor of Norway

Sweyn I Forkbeard [Sveinn, Svend] (*fl.* 987–1014): King of Denmark and briefly of England; father of Canute

Thorkell (*fl.* 1003–26): Viking leader, later Earl of East Anglia; served Sweyn Forkbeard, Canute and Ethelred

THE NORSEMEN

Eric of Norway (d. 1023): Earl of Northumbria; ally of Canute

Harald Hardrada (d. 1066): King of Norway and founder of Oslo; invaded England; slain at Stamford Bridge

Magnus (d. 1047): King of Norway; son of Olaf; Emma was accused of supporting his claim to the English throne

Olaf Haraldsson (d. 1030): Canute's rival for the throne of Norway; St Olaf of Norway

THE FLEMINGS

Baldwin V (d. 1067): Count of Flanders; descendant of Alfred the Great of Wessex; gave hospitality to many political refugees, including Emma

Matilda (d. 1083): Baldwin's daughter; wife of William the Conqueror

INTRODUCTION

One of the strangest sights in any of the great churches of England is in Winchester Cathedral, where four boxes, resembling houses with ornamentation of birds and angels, are placed high above the spectators' heads. They are mortuary chests, a term more usually associated with Egyptian pharaohs. Within them are jumbles of skulls and bones brought from a royal burial ground dating from the Saxon and Viking Ages of England. They include the remains of one woman, Emma of Normandy, twice Queen of England.

Further up the steep High Street, in the Great Hall above the cathedral, is another of Winchester's famous sights, King Arthur's Round Table. Arthur (if he existed) lived at the beginning and Emma near the end of an era, some six centuries long, that is little regarded by comparison with post-Conquest times. It includes the Vikings, those figures left over from the heroic pagan ages that the Church replaced with saints, martyrs, pilgrims and relics – holy bones, nails and dead tufts of hair.

Around King Arthur float the bright veils of Celtic legend or chivalric romance, or the more homespun attire of a Romano-British chieftain opposing the early Saxon invaders. The Vikings are always associated with ocean voyages and plundering raids, but they had another aspect, that of settlers in the English countryside and among town-dwelling Angles and Saxons. They wished to belong to the land the Romans had left to its original Celtic Britons. So this is the account of a people who tried to settle England and failed.

Queen Emma stands at the meeting point of the three cultures of the early Middle Ages: Saxon, Viking and Norman. A Viking by descent and sister of Richard, Duke of Normandy, she married Canute, the Dane who took the crown of England in 1016, when the Viking Age still had another fifty years to run. As Emma had previously been the wife of the Saxon Ethelred II (the Unready), she is the only woman to have married two kings of England. Her sons, Edward the Confessor and Hardecanute, were both kings in their turn.

Modern scholars have researched and expanded contemporary histories of the eleventh century, and Emma's several identities have been discussed at length in academic books. It has been argued that, in the context of her age, she was a powerful political figure. The Church's influence can hardly be overstated, and Emma was a generous benefactor. Her name appears prominently on a number of charters granting land. These facts are well documented and mean more than they seem at first reading. But another interpretation of her actions and motives could be that at heart she was a Danish nationalist who wished to see England joined not with Normandy but with Viking Denmark. As such, during her marriage to Ethelred she could have been a hidden part of the treachery that pervaded his court.

Unfortunately, one of the gaps in her life story is her relationship with Gunnor, her Danish mother, who was alive and in a position of some authority for years after Emma married Ethelred.

Like all queens, Emma's marital life was as significant as her public one. She was Ethelred's second wife and stepmother to a large family. Her experience of serial marriage was curious. Despite the efforts of the Church to regulate marriage, many couples entered into an arrangement known as a handfast union. It was more formal than the partnerships of today – and more respectable than concubinage (a handfast wife would have strongly objected to being referred to as a concubine) – but without the full approval of the Church.

Canute had made such a marriage before meeting Emma, and for many years she had to endure the presence of his handfast wife, Elgiva of Northampton. Like another royal marriage, this one must have been rather crowded with three people in it. Elgiva, said Canute, was not negotiable.

I have to say that I would much like to write the story of Elgiva, who shadowed Emma both as queen and as queen mother. Although marginalized, she had more political power than most queens, exerting it in Norway when it was part of Canute's realm and in England after his death. There seems no doubt that the love the otherwise unsympathetic Canute felt towards Elgiva was true and lasting. It is tempting to speculate on their first meeting and courtship, the births of their children, her feelings when he married Emma, their times together at Bosham in Sussex and whether she encouraged his un-Viking-like support of the Church. But that is the stuff of a novel, and this book, being based on thorough research, does not allow for such scenes.

Emma spent the last nine years of her life in retirement and, although she probably kept abreast of current events, took no active part in them. Her story continues through the reign of Edward the Confessor and his queen, Edith, sister of King Harold. It would seem that Emma's influence on their marriage was both strong and baleful.

But speculation extends further than that. Had Emma returned to Normandy and her children instead of marrying Canute and providing him with an heir, and had Edward and his younger brother Alfred come straight to England on Canute's death, Viking rule would have ended six years before it did. Alfred's murder and Edward's childless marriage left England without an heir and prey to the ambitions of the Norman William.

Of the documents detailing the age in which Emma lived, those collectively known as *The Anglo-Saxon Chronicles* were written between the late ninth century and Henry II's accession in 1154 by monks in Winchester, Canterbury, Abingdon, Worcester and Peterborough. They refer to Emma as 'the Lady', an Old English term, which had been used for King Alfred's wife, Ealhswith. I have used the Chronicles for the reigns that covered Emma's lifetime (seven if Sweyn Forkbeard and Edmund Ironside are counted). Other historians, mostly writing in the twelfth century, were those known as William of Malmesbury, Henry of Huntingdon and Florence of Worcester.

As well as these Old English or medieval Latin texts, there are the charters drawn up for land grants, also law codes and public records, of which far and away the most important is the survey known as the 'Domesday Book', which is kept in the Public Record Office, Kew. Other manuscripts, including books, have survived

and can be seen in the British Library in the Euston Road, London.

Without these, the period between the original Saxon settlements (probably in the fifth century), the first Viking raids (793) and the Norman Conquest would deserve the label of the Dark Ages. Work on this period, published in learned papers and academic books, is accessible to anyone interested. The full lists of texts I have consulted and museums I visited is given at the back of the book.

A new edition of *The Anglo-Saxon Chronicles*, with many enlightening footnotes, is available through mainstream bookshops, as is Sir Frank Stenton's *Anglo-Saxon England*, part of the 'Oxford History of England' series. This, the classic work on the age, is so comprehensive it is difficult to see how it could ever be bettered. Almost anything I needed to check, even when writing about Scandinavia, could be found there.

The dates given to many events of Emma's life are uncertain and the events themselves are known only in outline. This applies even to her marriages and coronations. There are often different versions of what was happening, both to her and to others. When in doubt, I have followed the account that seems to fit best into the rest of the narrative. It is most often that of Stenton.

As much personal detail of the lives of Emma and Edith as remains has been collected and interpreted by Professor Pauline Stafford, the leading expert on the queens, in *Queen Emma and Queen Edith: Queenship and Women's Power in Eleventh-Century England*.

There is no question that Stafford's is the most accurate picture of Emma ever likely to be written. But Emma has the distinction of having commissioned a book of her own on her years of marriage to Canute and its aftermath, under the Latin title of *Encomium Emmae Reginae* (the biography of Queen Emma). This has been translated and edited by the Royal Historical Society. Not many copies are available, but I was fortunate enough to find one in a second-hand bookshop in Bath. The text is full of fascinating details, particularly on the subject of Viking ships. The work seems a complete confirmation of Emma's Danish bias.

In 1981, Viking artefacts from both England and Denmark were brought together in a magnificent exhibition, *The Vikings in England and Their Danish Homeland*. Queen Margrethe II of Denmark and the Prince of Wales were patrons. This was shown in Denmark at the National Museum in Copenhagen, the Prehistoric Museum in Moesgård and in England at the Yorkshire Museum, York. Again, I was able to find one of the few copies of the catalogue still available, and it has been my best source for an overview of the Viking Age.

More archaeological information comes from Julian D. Richards's *Viking Age England* and the archives and museum services of various towns, especially Winchester.

I spent many hours with the *Dictionary of National Biography*. This Victorian edition, soon to be superseded, is invaluable for details of the lives of almost everyone I have mentioned. An exception was Gunhild, Emma and Canute's daughter, treated as a pawn by her father but surely with loving care as the baby by her mother. The *DNB* does not include an entry on her or her half-sister Goda, but the *Cambridge Medieval History* gives the details of Gunhild's sad fate.

A printed edition of *Encyclopaedia Britannica*, which I used during my six years as an editorial writer and sub-editor in its London office, was a necessary back-up. So was the CD-Rom version, *Britannica CD2000*, which has a much better article on Canute than the earlier one.

Visits to museums, cathedrals, abbeys and churches yielded a number of useful publications. Wiltshire County Council has issued an invaluable report, *A Millennium Tale*, with accompanying CD, which gives details of everyday life in Saxon times as well as the history. Additional detail came from the providers of illustrations.

From another viewpoint, I was particularly pleased with the discovery of the Cambridge University Library manuscript (Ee.3.59). Not only does it prove that Emma and Edward, Canute, Ironside and the rest were remembered in Plantagenet England, but they are shown in pictures like those in the kind of children's storybook that keeps alive tales of history and legend from a thousand years ago or more.

The greatest beneficiary of the Norman Conquest was the English language and its proper names. Emma, the epitome of the French quality of chic, did not appeal to the Saxons. They called Emma Aelfgifu, which fortunately can be latinized into Elgiva, as Godgifu becomes Godiva or Goda. I have also substituted Elfrida for Aelfthryth, Edith for Eadgyth, Alphege for Aelfheah. Canute, more accurately Cnut or Knutr, is preferred in the latest version of the *Encyclopaedia Britannica*. His and Emma's son is usually called Harthacnut or, worse still, Horthaknutr, but I call him Hardecanute, which is also the spelling used by the *EB*.

On the Norman side I have given Arlette rather than Herleva for Robert of Normandy's French concubine/handfast wife, mother of William the Conqueror and another marginalized woman with power. It was gratifying to find so many women playing significant parts in this narrative of the Viking Age.

I have called the king's *witan* the council, a *burh* a borough, the *fyrd* the militia and an *ealdorman* an earl (although, strictly speaking, earl derives from Old Norse *jarl*). But it seemed better not to attempt to find a modern equivalent of thane (more correctly *thegn*), the rank of a retainer of noble birth.

The image of Emma as a chess queen was suggested by the Lewis chess set in the British Museum, which was carved from walrus ivory some time in the twelfth century, after Emma's lifetime but when her people, the Normans, were dominant in continental Europe as well as England. The ivory queen wears a crown set on a short embroidered veil. Her right hand is against her cheek and the other hand supports her elbow. A long cloak opens over her robe.

But Emma was a wife, mother and widow as well as queen, a woman who made her mark on the age in which she lived.

It is appropriate, when writing of the distant past – even when it is Christian – to colour it with elements of legend and fairytale. History is a subject for children's imagination to work on, and I confess to having first made Emma's acquaintance in Charles Dickens's *A Child's History of England*; perhaps his least-known book, although it has been reprinted many times by many publishers. In particular, Dickens expounds on the St Brice's Day

Massacre, the treacherous deed that struck at England's heart and may have turned Emma against not only her Saxon husband but his children and people as well.

But my chief wish in writing this book is that it will help to bring Emma and those among whom she lived back to life and into what is perceived as mainstream history.

ETHELRED THE KING

In the year 1001, around the celebration of Christmas, King Ethelred II of England met his council in Kent to discuss a matter of importance. For once it was not a report that Vikings had landed on the south coast or were creeping through the Thames Estuary, the Medway or the Trent to burn, kill and plunder. A Viking fleet was anchored off the Isle of Wight, but its men were willing to wait for the twenty-four thousand pounds of silver they had been promised if they would sail home to Denmark, ruled by Sweyn, called Forkbeard.

The Saxon king and his council were not thinking of the dismal business of raising rents and taxes to pay the latest instalment of what came to be known as Danegeld. The subject under discussion was one that afforded at least some prospect of rejoicing. Ethelred had recently lost his wife, Elgiva, and the churchmen, earls and thanes of the council wished him to take a new wife.

Elgiva had borne Ethelred many children, but her company meant little to him compared with that of certain handsome and amusing young men in his court. As a widower he had hoped to be left with these favourites, but the council saw the opportunity to negotiate with a foreign ruler and make an alliance to protect England more effectively. However much money the Vikings were given, they always seemed likely to return.

The council knew as well as Ethelred himself that the Vikings would have stayed away had the fleets sent by his father, King Edgar, to patrol the northern coasts of England not been left in harbour by Ethelred. Spies and sailors from ships blown off their courses reported to the Norwegians (Norsemen) and Danes that coastal settlements were unguarded. Norway and Denmark were not yet fully Christian. Underlying discontent with the closing of pagan temples led to unrest, and unrest to raiding parties on undefended England.

These raids had been the habit of the Vikings of the North for more than two hundred years, varying in success according to the character and ability of whoever was king in England at the time. Often the raiders were small in number but still too many for the people of the settlements or monasteries of the coast to resist. In 997, however, many more ships had arrived, with the intention of stripping the south coast and southern Wales of such assets as silver plate, manuscripts, woollen cloth and horses. After three years of this, they went to winter in Normandy, where the people were descended from Vikings themselves and willing to buy the plunder taken from England. The Vikings then returned across the Channel to hold the Saxons to ransom.

Ethelred and his council had drawn up a list of terms under which both English king and Norman duke (Emma's father) should agree to repair any injuries each might inflict on the other and neither give shelter to the other's enemies. Duke Richard had agreed to the terms, but the Vikings continued to raid England. At the council in 1001, therefore, it was proposed that Ethelred should marry Emma, great-granddaughter of the original Viking founder of Normandy and sister of the present Duke Richard.

There were princesses in France and Germany and the great city of Constantinople, and the King of England, when his country was at peace, was a match for any of them. But a Norman marriage alliance would compel the duke to take firm action against the Vikings. This argument overcame Ethelred's reluctance. He agreed that an embassy should be sent to Normandy to ask Emma's brother for her hand.

Emma's father had died five years earlier. Her mother, Gunnor, had first been his handfast wife. She produced a large family, and the union became a full marriage in about 989. Gunnor had been born a Dane and remained one at heart. Emma was almost entirely Scandinavian by blood and probably by inclination, too.

Her brothers and sisters, nephews and nieces, when they did not hold high positions in the Church, married into the duchies and countships of France. Emma's first daughter was to make two French marriages.

But Duke Richard, listening to the Saxon embassy in his castle at Rouen, was willing to turn his eyes towards England. The united kingdom of Wessex in the south, Mercia (the Midlands and East Anglia) and Northumbria in the north was rich. Its meadowlands supported flocks of sheep; shiploads of English wool crossed the Channel and in return silver flowed like a river from the mines in the Harz mountains of the German Empire. It would be good to think that a nephew of the Duke of Normandy would one day be king of the country. Regrettably, that looked hardly possible, as Ethelred already had six sons in line for the throne.

Nevertheless, Emma's position in England as its queen would

be better than in Normandy, where she counted for little compared with her sister-in-law, Judith of Brittany, its duchess. She would have her own income from land which she could dispose of as she pleased. As the key figure in the alliance between Normandy and England, she might have what so few women achieved, real political power.

To both brother and sister the prospect was a desirable one. Acceptance of the proposal was sent to Ethelred, who authorized payment of the bride price and entered into further negotiations, this time for Emma's dowry.

Because almost nothing is known of Emma's upbringing, education – although she knew Latin – and family relationships, it is impossible to speculate on how the girl she was before marriage influenced the woman she became after marriage. By contrast, her husband Ethelred's background is well documented.

His father, Edgar, had had three children. His daughter, called by the favourite Saxon name of Edith, died young and was reverenced as a saint – not an uncommon thing to happen to kings' daughters placed in nunneries. She was the child of a handfast marriage to Wulfrid, a novice at the nunnery at Wilton, near Salisbury. Edgar took another handfast wife, Ethelfleda, the daughter of one of his earls, but was often unfaithful to her, even though the child she bore him was a son, Edward.

East Anglia was ruled by Edgar's friend, Earl Ethelwold. He brought to court his wife, Elfrida, a woman so good-looking that Edgar's nobles advised her husband to tell her to appear in tattered rags, wearing no ornaments and with her hair uncombed, to avoid attracting the notice of the king. Shortly afterwards, Ethelwold died.

It was said that Edgar had heard of Elfrida's beauty when she was a young girl and sent Ethelwold to report back to him. The earl was dazzled by her and married her, telling Edgar the reports of her beauty were false. She put on her best finery when she came to court, and the king, seeing her, ordered her husband's death.

This is an unlikely story, for Elfrida was not a girl of humble birth who made her way by sexual allure alone. She was the daughter of the Earl of Devon. Her success in meeting and fulfilling the king's needs was such that Edgar threw all caution to the winds, and the death of Earl Ethelwold was ascribed to the atmosphere of adulterous passion.

When Edgar died suddenly, Elfrida had claimed the throne for their son Ethelred, but the council followed the advice of Dunstan, Archbishop of Canterbury and Edgar's chief minister, and chose Edward instead. After three years, Edward had been assassinated on a visit to Elfrida and Ethelred at Corfe, the highest point of the Isle of Purbeck in Dorset.

Ethelred could remember seeing his mother's serving man approach Edward as he sat on his horse, the sudden flash of a dagger and the cry of the king. The horse had bolted, with Edward entangled in the reins, feet caught in the stirrups, rushing downhill out of sight. Elfrida had seized a wand from one of the servants and beaten her shocked son soundly with it, threatening him with more strokes if he told the council what he had seen.

The body of Edward had been taken in haste to Wareham, the nearest mainland town, and buried without ceremony. There was an outcry throughout the land, not only on account of the manner of his death but also the scandal of no one coming forward to avenge it.

Dunstan had crowned Ethelred king. Then, unexpectedly, he came with Earl Elfhere of Mercia and the Abbess of Wilton to Wareham to find the body of Edward.

They were shown the grave, and when it was opened Dunstan declared the body to be incorrupt, the sign of sainthood. In the sandy soil of Dorset this might have been true, and no one would venture to challenge Dunstan. The body was sealed in a coffin covered with an embroidered cloth. It was then loaded on to a cart and conveyed to the abbey of Shaftesbury for requiem mass and reburial.

It would seem that, although Elfrida the Queen set the trap, the hand that struck down Edward was that of a servant of Earl Elfhere. The king became known as 'the Martyr', and his relics were revered. Elfrida later went to live on one of her own estates. Rumour said she wished to avoid the sight of her son's follies and repented conspiring to murder Edward for Ethelred's sake.

The difficulties which lay before Emma did not include Elfrida, who had died two years before the marriage alliance with Normandy. Ethelred had granted lands to the Church for the repose of her soul. But the psychological effect of witnessing Edward's murder was what made Ethelred, about thirty-three years of age at the time of his second marriage, the man he was. His people had the additional misfortune that the council which could have made up his deficit frequently included the treacherous and the incompetent. As a result, although his name means 'noble counsel', he has become known as 'the Unready' or, more correctly, 'lacking good counsel' and as such is remembered today.

Emma was about fifteen years his junior and altogether unschooled in matters of state when she came to England to be queen. The preparations for her journey and her marriage would have included learning English, in addition to Norman French and the Danish she spoke with her mother.

There was much excitement among the Saxons waiting to escort the girl known as 'the Flower of Normandy' for her beauty. Many years ago, before any of them were born, King Athelstan had married Edgiva, one of his sisters, to that king of France who had granted Vikings the territory that became the dukedom of Normandy. The Duke of the Franks (after whom France is named) had asked for another sister, Edhild, for his wife. The gifts he had sent to Athelstan were still spoken of for their richness and sanctity – jewels, a vase made of onyx and relics of Christ the Son of Mary himself. Another of Athelstan's sisters, Edith, had been married to Otto, the German king who after her death had been crowned emperor. But the Saxon kings usually married – or entered into handfast marriage with – high-born ladies of their own land.

Once married, there was no question of Emma being merely an ornament or object of veneration. Although she would come to the actual palace only when summoned, she would be active in the life of the court, presiding over it as Mary presided over the court of heaven. She would supervise its many removals from one great hall to another throughout the kingdom. She would see that the king appeared in robes that marked him out above all others and herself solve any domestic problems. She would be the hostess who made certain her guests lacked for nothing and saw to it that the chamberlains and stewards of the court were rewarded for their toils. She would select gifts according to the merits of those who were to receive them. She would mark who were the men of influence in Ethelred's kingdom and maintain friendly and tactful relations with them. She would have to be be devout and generous to the Church and, if necessary, remind the king of his duty to it. And she would have to remain constant in loyalty and respect to her husband, looking on his family and people as her own and treating his actions and behaviour as above reproach. Despite the existing family, she should bear children and hope that any who died were girls not boys.

The Church spoke of love between husband and wife in terms of the patriarchs of ancient Israel – Abraham and Sarah, Isaac and Rebecca. Emma's own father had loved her mother, Gunnor, making her his true wife when he could have set her aside. For Emma, being sent to marry a foreigner much older than herself, there was only hope. But, at the very least, the English king would surely value her as the representative of what England at that time was not: an efficient military state.

So the day came for the uncomfortable journey across the Channel and the marriage to Ethelred. A number of French and Breton attendants went with Emma to relieve her homesickness. The behaviour of one of these, a man called Hugh, was to confirm a suspicion held by some Saxons that the new queen favoured the Danish invaders of the kingdom.

It could, of course, be argued that this was hardly surprising. To Emma, the yellow-haired men with blue sailors' eyes and the smell of the sea about them whom she had known in Rouen were friends, kinsmen even, made welcome for the wealth they brought to Normandy. It would take a complete change of mindset to see them as enemies and herself as a weapon to use against them.

She arrived during Lent, those six weeks before Easter when Christians give up feasting and merrymaking. This suited the mood of the king. At the insistence of his council he had banished his favourite, Leofsige, who had negotiated the latest payment to the Danes. During this mission Leofsige had killed Ethelred's chief officer, being jealous of his promotion.

Emma probably landed at Sandwich on the Kent coast, like most other visitors from the Continent, including those heading for the port of London. The king's bride and her party were escorted to Canterbury, where the English Church was centred, even through the storms of the Viking Age. It was to Canterbury that the missionary Augustine had come from Rome in 597 to preach the true word of Christ in a land where many people were still pagan.

The name of the archbishop who was to marry Ethelred and Emma with the full rites of the Church was Elfric. The great Dunstan had died fourteen years before.

Whatever else in the way of speech and customs was strange to Emma, she was on familiar ground with the Church. Inspired by a similar movement in France, Dunstan, with the Bishops Ethelwold of Winchester and Oswald of York, had led the first Reformation in England. They restored monasteries destroyed by the Danes and founded new ones, work which lasted until the more thorough Reformation under Henry VIII.

When Emma was presented to Ethelred, the portents seemed hopeful. As one of the chroniclers of his time put it, he was 'good-looking and of graceful manners, no means deficient in ability or especially slothful'. Later would come the discovery that he was 'impulsive, passionate, cruel and apt to lean on favourites, whom he did not choose for any worthy reasons; he had no principles of action and was guided by motives of temporary expediency'.

The marriage ceremony was combined with the rite of coronation. First there was the nuptial mass, when Ethelred and Emma were joined in a partnership signifying the union of Christ and his Church. On earth this partnership was for peace, health, children and preparation for eventual entry into heaven.

Then Emma prostrated herself before the altar and was raised by bishops who prayed over her. She was anointed on the head with oil to dedicate her to God. A ring completed the process and wedded her to both Ethelred and his kingdom.

Lastly, the archbishop set a crown on Emma's head, so that she became an object of reverence, a creature of glory and delight, lifted above the pain, humiliation, fear and anxieties that are the usual lot of women. Crowned and clad in linen and jewelled embroidery, her wedding ring on her hand, she had changed from featureless pawn to queen, and England was now her chessboard.

After the feasting and celebration came the other rite, more – although not altogether – private, which made her Ethelred's wife in the flesh. The nature of that relationship cannot be known. Altogether she was to bear five children.

The morning after her wedding night she was told of the gifts assigned to her: the profits of a number of towns, including

Winchester, capital of the Saxon kings, and Exeter in Devon; also land in Northamptonshire and all west Suffolk. These profits were collected by officers known as reeves, and Emma appointed the Frenchman Hugh to Exeter.

Thus the daughter of Vikings began to amass riches in England, long regarded as the rightful prey of Vikings. For his part, her brother Richard contacted Sweyn of Denmark with an offer of peace, a blind eye to be turned to Vikings in Normandy and more sale of plunder.

In the world of the imagination, which may bridge the lands of the physical world, certain kings from Denmark ruled over England. One, Havelok, was thrown out of his kingdom as a child and brought up in the English kingdom of Lindsey, now part of Lincolnshire, by a fisherman called Grim, after whom Grimsby is named. The adventures of Havelok and how he was restored to his kingdom were told in both French and the Lincolnshire dialect.

Another Dane, Angys, conquered Britain at the behest of Fortager, who had driven the rightful heir, Uther Pendragon, into exile in Brittany. On Uther's return, he marched on Winchester and, with the help of Merlin the magician, drove out both Fortager and Angys the Dane. This Uther was the father of King Arthur.

Olger, or Ogier the Dane, is the hero of a Celtic tale found in the romances of the life of Charlemagne, the French emperor whose realm had by the eleventh century been split into France and Germany. Ogier became King of Britain and in old age was carried away by the enchantress Morgan le Fay.

Before the first versions of these legends were blown on the winds between Denmark and Britain, an account of the distant lands of the North appeared in a translation of the fifth-century *Histories* of Orosius. According to a Norseman called Ohthere, money and taxes were paid in those lands in deerskins, feathers, walrus skins and seals. Taxes were set according to rank, the wealthiest having to pay fifteen marten furs, five reindeer hides, one bearskin, a cloak of bear or otter skin, ten measures of feathers and two ropes for ships.

Because the northern land was long and narrow, men could plough and pasture herds only along the less rocky parts of the coastline. It was the isolation and poverty of the North that brought about the growth of a culture based on the mastery of the sea rather than the building of cities. Freed from the constraints of rulers and the disease and fighting that often break out inside city walls, the Vikings developed a psychology that assured them that the possessions of people in the wealthier lands to the south were theirs for the taking. And they did take them, to an extent that brought the Christian civilization growing up on the ruins of the Roman Empire close to collapse.

The instruments by which they accomplished this were their distinctive ships, poetically called 'wave stallions'. They were long and narrow, some with draughts shallow enough to enable them to go up estuaries and large rivers and approach close to shore. They had holds for cargo, oars, including one for steering, and tall pine masts with square sails. The masts could be lowered. Streamers of three-sided wind vanes attached to the prows or others shaped like birds and fastened to the masts showed the speed of the wind, and both prows and sterns were carved into figureheads. Often the whole ship was decorated with figures of beasts.

Two years before Emma came to England, a man called Leif Ericsson sailed to the far west in search of cod fisheries. While the Saxons were struggling to hold England against the Danes, Norsemen were trying to establish colonies in the lands of modern North America and Greenland.

Against Viking ships, those of the Saxons were like ducks compared with swans. The boats used on rivers such as the Thames and the Lea were hollowed-out tree-trunks. They were to convey farm produce, for fishing or reed-cutting expeditions or to carry a few passengers. The sailing ships that took longer journeys up rivers or crossed the Channel or the North Sea were clinker-built.

But the Vikings were not only superior on the sea. They were also tremendous horsemen, who shod their horses' hooves with iron and rode them with stirrups of iron and brass wire, snaffle-bits (bridles) and cheek pieces. As many horses as their ships could carry were brought across the North Sea.

The Vikings differed from the other peoples of western Europe during the eighth to tenth centuries in another supremely important respect: they were pagans. Their chief gods were Odin and Thor. Odin, known as the All-Father, was the god of battle in whose hall, Valhalla, the souls of warriors slain that day were waited on at great feasts by maidens called Valkyries. The raven, the bird of Odin, appeared on banners carried into battle. Odin was also the master of wisdom and magic, and thus related to shamans or witch doctors. Thor was the thunder god, a red-bearded figure who carried a hammer and protected both the gods themselves and humankind, especially voyagers.

The Vikings did not think their gods were immortal and would live until the end of time. They told of Ragnarok or *Götterdämmerung*, Richard Wagner's 'Twilight of the Gods'. One by one the gods will be killed in a battle with giants and monsters, and both earth and heaven be destroyed with fire. Then will come a form of resurrection, with a new green earth appearing from the sea, to be repopulated by a man and woman who had hidden in the world tree, the great ash Yggdrasil, until Ragnarok was over.

This myth is an expression of the concept of fate that cannot be averted, similar in principle to the Christian notion of the will of God. In the Old English of the Saxons it is known as *wyrd*.

It was the Franks, the people of Charlemagne, who first broke down the isolation of Denmark and Norway. The Franks conquered the Frisians, North Sea people who are among the ancestors of the English. They then made a new northern frontier, and the Danes responded by building a mighty rampart, the Danevirke, which still exists, between the Baltic and the North Sea. Behind this rampart towns and trading ports grew up, one being Roskilde on the island of Zealand.

The balance of power between the Danes and Franks was maintained until Charlemagne's empire broke up under his successors. Then the Danes began to raid the Frankish lands and Denmark itself fell into anarchy after the slaying of the king and princes by a claimant to the throne.

Now the Danes began to look further afield, along with the

Norse Vikings. Their voyages were highly profitable. In particular, they robbed and destroyed abbeys, in which articles of precious materials and fine workmanship, once hidden in pagan graves, were offered for the greater glory of God. But it has been argued that the Vikings did the settled peoples a service by bringing so much wealth back into circulation.

The Vikings were skilled smiths, especially in silver, which was the basis of their portable wealth. They displayed it on their persons in the form of rings for arms and fingers, some being made of twisted strands of wire, and brooches, some very large or in the form of thistleheads, and amulets with punched decoration. Another design was of animals with ribbon bodies, like sea creatures. They also made beads and finger rings of green and yellow glass as well as jet and amber jewellery.

Early in the Viking Age, silver items were cut up into what was called hack silver, which was valued by weight. The northern settlers of England were the first to strike coins in quantity. Some were stamped with a bird design, the raven of Odin.

The overseas voyages and raids of the summer months – the ships were laid up for winter – were better than today's football matches for young Vikings needing to burn up surplus energy in adventure and excitement. After a while, however, the long days at sea, cold and dangerous even in summertime, would begin to pall. They looked for land to take and colonize, where they could reap far more bushels of grain than in the cold climate of their homelands.

In about 840, Norse Vikings made a settlement that became Dublin. They also turned to the continent of Europe. There were many abbeys in France, and Viking ships slid like knives into its heart, along the rivers Loire, Garonne and Seine. Eventually the French king known as Charles the Simple gave up trying to beat off a great band of Vikings under a chief called Rollo, and in 911 the lands round the mouth of the Seine, together with Rouen, were granted to the Vikings by treaty.

More arrived, and by the time Rollo's great-grandson, Emma's brother Richard, was duke, additional territory had been acquired. Emma's grandfather, William Longsword, annexed the Channel Islands, now the only part of Normandy under the English crown. The dukes of Normandy ruled like kings. As pottery is made from clay and carvings from stone, so from the Vikings came a new people, hard, competent, disciplined, destined to be the masters of England and dominant in southern Italy and Sicily.

The Vikings known in England were of three types: the Danes who settled Northumbria and Mercia in the ninth century; the Norsemen from Dublin and the islands of Scotland; and those who came in fleets straight from Denmark and Norway.

They became familiar with the inlets and bays of the coasts of England, Wales and the land of the Scots. They discovered the estuaries, Thames, Medway, Trent, Humber and Severn, up which they could penetrate inland. Some estuaries have islands, notably Sheppey, off Kent, where the first Danish invaders landed.

The Vikings found large rocks and islets in the British seas, the homes of seabirds, with the occasional hermit seeking his god in wind and tide beneath the stars. On major islands – some, such as Wight, close to shore; others, like Man, far out to sea – invaders landed to colonize or set up bases for attacks. Man was settled by

Norsemen; Wight was the base from which Vikings raided Wessex. Far to the north, in the islands of Orkney, Shetland and the Hebrides, Norsemen set themselves up as sea kings and earls. And to the west lay Ireland and the Norse settlement of Dublin, which presented a considerable threat to England. Indeed, nothing less than a cordon thrown round all the coasts could keep away a determined seafaring enemy.

It was such an enemy, a troop of up to a thousand men, whose military skill and determination made them seem many more, that landed in East Anglia from Denmark in 865 both to take the usual plunder and to gain territory. They managed to seize enough horses to ride through Mercia and into the northern province, Northumbria, and conquer its chief city, York. Their weapons were longswords, axes with cutting edges and firebrands, topped with flame struck from steel by flint.

Three years later, the King of Mercia and his council sent to Wessex to ask help against the Danes, who were wintering at Nottingham. The name of the King of Wessex was Ethelred, and the brother who accompanied him was called Alfred.

Below the cathedral in Winchester an imposing statue of King Alfred, holding his sword hilt to form a cross, faces up the High Street. The image is often used as a logo by Hampshire charities, but it is mostly visitors to the historic city who pause to look at the statue itself. But, although he was king only of Wessex, Alfred's rule defined England. In the face of enemies he seized his hour, as Churchill and Elizabeth I did theirs, and he bestrides his times like a colossus. If anyone is asked why the Saxon and Viking Ages should be remembered after more than nine centuries, the shortest and most conclusive reply is the name of Alfred.

With his brother Ethelred, Alfred led an army to Reading against the Danes, but they were defeated. Other battles followed, and a fresh contingent of Danes arrived by sea. In 871 Ethelred died from wounds, and Alfred, aged twenty-two and with a young wife, Ealhswith, became King of Wessex, seemingly with little likelihood of withstanding the Danes. *The Anglo-Saxon Chronicles* tell of battles across Wessex and Mercia and how the Danes wintered at a town called Lundenwic or London, to which pottery, including wine jars, and millstones were brought up the Thames from northern France and the Rhineland.

Providence seemed to be on Alfred's side when a Danish fleet ran into a storm and many ships were wrecked in the great harbour of Poole on the south coast. Alfred pursued the raiders and their horses as far as Exeter, and peace was made with the swearing of oaths. But the oaths were broken, and the Danes overran first Mercia and then Wessex to such effect that Alfred and a handful of followers were driven through woodland into the marshes of Somerset. Here they fortified the island of Athelney and made guerrilla raids against the Danes in the wet countryside round about.

In the early summer of 878, Alfred, having drawn Saxons and the Britons of the west together, led his troop to Edington in Wiltshire against the Danes and their king, Guthrum. The invaders were defeated, and Guthrum came to Alfred to make terms.

The peace was too fragile for Alfred to do other than offer large concessions. What the Danes wanted was a sizeable portion of the English land off which they had been living. If this was granted them, they would plough and sow it and pasture cattle, horses and flocks of sheep with wool as dense and soft as the English grass they cropped.

Guthrum's power base was in East Anglia, but his authority extended into south Mercia. The part of what is known as the Danelaw granted him by Alfred was divided from Wessex by the rivers Lea and Thames and by Watling Street. This, the greatest of the roads left by the Romans, runs from east Kent through London and the Midlands to Shropshire and the border of Wales. It is still in use, although usually under different names – for instance, High Street, Rochester.

Alfred acknowledged that the treaty meant that two different races, Mercians and Danes, would be living side by side. Equality was guaranteed by law. Five towns – Lincoln, Stamford, Derby, Nottingham and Leicester – became distinctly Danish in character and were known as the Five Boroughs.

Now it was Alfred's turn to make a demand, in his eyes one at least as significant as the granting of territory. It was that Guthrum and his followers should be baptized and become members of the Army of God. The organization of archbishops and bishops in their sees held the Christian community together and made back-sliding difficult. The hub, of course, was Rome, but Hamburg in Germany was the missionary centre for the northern lands.

The missionaries brought with them a new skill, that of writing with pen and paper. Previously, Viking written records had consisted only of brief statements in the lettering known as runes, cut into stone or wood.

Guthrum agreed to baptism, in return for much wealth, and the ceremony was performed at the village of Wedmore in Somerset. But there were more Viking raids in the south, and King Alfred occupied London. After four years of attacks the enemy withdrew.

Alfred rebuilt towns and founded new ones, called boroughs, during his Danish campaigns. Some boroughs were on sites used by the Romans and, earlier still, by Iron Age people. (Roman towns had stone walls which, after rebuilding or repair, afforded better protection than the wooden palisades of the Saxons.)

Alfred, having designed ships to guard against further coastal raids, which has earned him the title of 'Father of the English Navy', turned to administration, lawgiving and education, including literacy in Old English. Many visitors came to his court, and it was Alfred who inserted the traveller's tale of Ohthere in the *Histories* of Orosius.

Another ancient writer who attracted Alfred's attention was the philosopher Boethius. He used his pagan writings to illuminate the problem of *wyrd*. Although evil in itself, fate can yet be defeated by philosophy and Christian teaching.

It is not known whether Emma was able to apply this high-minded principle to the events of her own life. Alfred died in 899, a hundred and three years before she came to England, but his name had a tragic resonance throughout her later years.

Alfred's successor was the first of the eleven Edwards who have been proclaimed king in England (the fifth and eighth were not crowned). To Ethelred, the name, that of his murdered elder brother, would have been somewhat ill-omened. To Emma it was ambivalent.

This first Edward, called the Elder – who reigned between 899 and 924 – was a great warrior king whose capabilities were soon tested. The Viking settlers in Northumbria had not altogether given up their old way of life and pagan values. Edward sent an army against them and fighting extended into Mercia, until the English won a major victory at Tettenhall in Staffordshire.

Mercia at this time was ruled by one Ethelred. Alfred had made him governor of the new town and port that he had founded on the Thames. As well as traces of eighth-century Lundenwic, remembered in the name Aldwych (old town), Museum of London archaeologists have discovered quays and streets between the Thames and Cheapside dating from Alfred's time or a little later.

Ethelred of Mercia, Governor of London, was married to King Edward's older sister, Ethelfleda. She, as well as Edward, inherited much of their father's abilities and charisma and after her husband's death was able to bring them into play. Known as 'the Lady of the Mercians', Ethelfleda led her militia on to the battlefield. She also followed her father in fortifying boroughs, he to defend Wessex, she to guard the part of Mercia not settled by the Danes.

The combined campaigns of Edward and Ethelfleda eventually made the Danes subject to the English king. But in 918, when Norsemen from Dublin were invading Northumbria, Ethelfleda died suddenly. Mercia was inherited by her daughter Elfwyn, who attracted the notice of the Viking King of York.

Rather than allow all Mercia to become Danish through a

marriage alliance, Edward directed that the heiress Elfwyn should be kidnapped. She disappeared into Wessex, presumably into a nunnery, and Mercia became, like Wessex, part of the English kingdom. It was during Edward the Elder's reign that a little village in south Mercia grew into Oxford.

Since the mid-seventh century, Winchester had been the centre of a bishop's see, the early cathedral being the church of the Old Minster, a monastery now outlined in stone in the grass north of today's cathedral.

Ethelwold, Bishop of Winchester, had been, with Dunstan, one of the prime movers of the tenth-century Benedictine Reformation. Ethelwold's reforming ire was roused by the discovery that the Old Minster was full of clerics living worldly lives, some with handfast wives, hardly bothering even to celebrate mass. With the help of Wulfstan, one of King Edgar's chief thanes, Ethelwold forced the community to give way to Benedictine monks from Abingdon. His was rewarded with an attempt to poison him at dinner; his survival was put down to his religious faith.

Ethelwold is remembered chiefly for the honour he wished to render his predecessor, Swithun, whose bones lay in the forecourt of the Old Minster. The humble burial had been the saint's own wish, but Ethelwold was not deterred from his plan. A splendid shrine was built for Swithun inside the church of the Old Minster, but Ethelwold moved his bones before it was finished.

The fifteenth of July, the saint's own day, was chosen for the exhumation. The bishop led the ceremony in his finest robes, attended by a train of monks and singers. Overhead the sky turned black. By the time the coffin had been lifted, the clerical robes were soaked with streaming rain and claps of thunder interrupted the chanting. Later it was said that the rain had lasted a full forty days and it was a marvel the world had not been flooded as in the days of Noah. Swithun, it was also said, was reading his successor at Winchester a lesson in humility.

Nine years later the saint's bones were moved in the presence of Ethelred to their final resting place. But not all the pomp and ceremony could eradicate the memory of what had happened earlier.

> St Swithun's day, if thou dost rain
> For forty days it will remain.

But the shrine did brisk business in miraculous healings. A great west front, comprising two towers and a spire, was erected round it. This was begun in Ethelwold's time but completed by his successor, Alphege, who was himself destined to be martyred by the Danes.

Another church, with only a narrow passageway between the two, was the New Minster, founded by Alfred and completed by Edward the Elder. Both are believed to have been buried there, with earlier kings, but all the graves have since been lost. Ealhswith, Alfred's wife, founded the nunnery later known as St Mary's Abbey.

Winchester was originally a well-built, well-tended Roman city called Venta Belgarum, after the Belgic tribe of Britons. Its significance in Saxon times began with the Old Minster, but it also became economically important after the decline of Hamwic

(Southampton), which was plundered by Vikings in the ninth century. Only the High Street now survives from Winchester's Roman street plan. The other streets were laid out in Alfred's reign, and people would have been able to follow the Roman wall by a Saxon street that ran alongside it. Many thousands of flint cobblestones went into road surfacing. The area between the streets was first divided into large estates which were later sliced up into properties about ten metres wide, as are many Winchester properties today. Houses had access to the High Street from the front and to two back streets from the rear.

The High Street was Winchester's chief trading area. People went to shops and stalls in specified areas for their goods, and the streets were named accordingly: there was Tanners' Street, Fleshmongers' (butchers) Street (now Parchment Street), the Fishmarket, Shoemakers' Street (now Jewry Street), Goldsmiths' Street and Shieldmakers' Street.

The making of woollen cloth was the main industry. It included spinning and weaving, much of which was done in the home, dyeing and fulling (cleansing and thickening the cloth). Bone needles, loom weights, spindle whorls and fulling stones can be seen in Winchester City Museum.

Between the markets and Shoemakers' Street – which lie at right angles to each other – is the estate that belonged to Emma. Her residence, known as a tenement, was at least two storeys tall, which was unusual before the late eleventh century. The tenement was known as Godbegot, a corruption of '[Elfric's] good bargain'.

Emma lived a self-sufficient life here, confiding in French to her servants or discussing the events of the day with visitors to Winchester. She intervened no more than other Saxon queens in the affairs of the kingdom, but the suspicion that she had plotted behind the closed doors of Godbegot contributed much later to her enforced retirement from public life.

It is not difficult to imagine the everyday details of Emma's life.

She would have worn linen, silk and the best English wool, made up into undergarments, overgarments with hoods, sleeved gowns and cloaks, some of them edged with braid. For the colder weather she had furs, the finest being from Russia, bought through the Varangian traders, Swedish cousins of the Vikings.

Her table was supplied with lamb and goose from the farmlands belonging to Winchester. Hunters in the nearby woodland provided venison, and snares were set for hare, pigeon and woodcock. Tender suckling pigs were taken from the enormous herds that, under the eyes of swineherds, fed on beechnuts and acorns in the woods. Fish and oysters were brought from the coast and eels from the ponds of water mills. Onions, leeks, cabbages and root vegetables were the accompaniments.

The food was served sometimes on English pottery, sometimes on pieces with abstract patterns from France and the Rhineland. The English ware might be made in Winchester itself: it had a yellow glaze, as did Stamford ware from Lincolnshire. Thetford ware from East Anglia was hard and grey. Between courses, silver bowls were brought round for hands to be rinsed. Knives and spoons, often of bone, were used.

At Emma and Ethelred's tables, wine from France and honeyed

mead were drunk from silver cups or horns. Curds, whey and buttermilk were available, by-products from cheese- and butter-making.

Time left after Emma's many duties would be spent in her bower, a small detached room, practising the art of embroidery for which Saxon women were renowned throughout Europe. Stitches of silk from Constantinople, fine wool and gold thread went into making robes for kings and princes and, for the Church, altar cloths as well as copes and chasubles, the garments worn by senior churchmen at mass.

For companions of her own rank with whom to practise her English, Emma had three stepdaughters, Edith, Wulfhild and Elgiva, the last being the name by which Emma herself was known to the Saxons. They were reserved for marriages to earls, a defence against treachery to Ethelred.

Their brothers lived like any other band of noble youths and boys, attending monastic schools and spending their leisure hours horse-racing, hawking or hunting stags and wild boar with dogs brought from Ireland.

Ethelred had named his sons after earlier kings: Athelstan, Egbert, Edmund, Edred, Edwy and Edgar. The first Egbert – grand-father of Alfred and who died in 839 – had done much to establish the eventually unshakeable position of Wessex among the English regions. He annexed the counties of Sussex, Surrey, Kent and Essex and, by a victory over the West Welsh (Cornish), who had joined forces with a troop of invading Danes, made Cornwall also part of Wessex.

Ethelred's other sons were called after the line of kings that extends from Edward the Elder to Ethelred himself. Edward the Elder's son and successor, Athelstan (d. 939), was also a mighty warrior, who became overlord of Scottish and Welsh princes and in 937 was the victor of the great battle of Brunanburh. But the Viking Age was not yet over. Athelstan's young half-brother, Edmund, later known as the Magnificent, had to deal with an invasion by Norse Vikings from Dublin. King Edmund was obliged to give up much of Danish Mercia, although he regained it later. He was fast proving himself to be the king England needed when he was killed in 946 by an armed robber in a brawl at a feast. Edred, his brother, who succeeded him as king, had been in poor health since childhood. Yet he led armies against the Norseman, Eric Bloodaxe, who had made York a Viking kingdom. After his defeat, wild and remote Northumbria, bordering on Scotland, came under the rule of the king, who was based at Winchester.

Edred's nine-year reign was followed by that of Edwy the Fair, the handsome but feckless son of Edmund. Edwy cared for nothing but hunting, feasting and the love of his young wife, Elgiva, for whose sake he had banished Dunstan, then Abbot of Glastonbury, who had caught them embracing during Edwy's coronation feast.

Tiring of Edwy, the great men of Mercia and Northumbria rose against him and chose his brother, Edgar, as their king. Edwy was left only with Wessex, and on his sudden, unexplained death in 959 Edgar became the King of England.

Dunstan, his minister, whom he made Archbishop of Canterbury, arranged for Edgar a coronation more splendid than any English king had had before. Kingston-upon-Thames was where earlier kings – and later Edward the Martyr and Ethelred –

were crowned (the coronation stone can still be seen in the Guildhall complex there). Edgar's coronation at Bath, the city of the Romans, echoed the crowning by which the German King Otto II had been made emperor by the Pope. Edgar and his successors had been bound yet more closely to the Church and their persons made sacrosanct. This coronation laid down the pattern for all others that followed in England.

Edgar, known as 'the Peaceful', ruled as administrator, lawgiver and reformer. Understanding that everyday confirmation of kingship is the coinage that carries the king's name and his image, he created a national currency and brought it under his own control. Every six years, old coins and foreign ones were melted down and struck again to a new design. A charge was paid to the king at each new minting. The striking of false money was punished by cutting off the forger's hand.

During the time of Edgar, Harald, called Bluetooth, brought all Denmark under his rule, claimed Norway and made Christianity the official religion of his realm. As a result, except for a rebellion in Northumbria, peace marked Edgar's reign. He had time to make laws under which Saxons, Angles, Britons and Danes should live in harmony. Law courts met every four weeks in the Saxon hundreds, which were divisions of the administrative districts called shires. The Danes had their own version, the wapentake. This word originally described the brandishing of weapons when an assembly came to a decision – like raising hands, only more emphatic. It then came to mean a grouping of villages for the purposes of lawgiving in the counties of the Five Boroughs of Lincoln, Stamford, Leicester, Nottingham and Derby and the North and

West Ridings of the old county of Yorkshire. (Riding means 'third part'. The East Riding still exists, but the North and West Ridings are now North and West Yorkshire respectively.) But, whereas in the hundreds the king and his council dealt with powerful men who broke the law, in the wapentakes the punishment was that due under Danish law.

'This self-government', said Edgar, 'is your reward for the fidelity you have always shown me.' Nothing marks the difference between him and his son Ethelred more starkly than this statement.

In the year 975, only two years after his and Elfrida's grand coronation, King Edgar died suddenly. His son Edward was murdered on a March day at Corfe. *Wyrd* was indeed still present in the land. It followed the kings' young namesakes, Emma's stepsons, neither of whom was destined to live beyond his twenties.

As queen, Emma found herself greeting and entertaining more people than she might have expected while still in her Norman home. Besides the Mercians and Northumbrians from the Midlands and north of the kingdom, she met Welsh, Scots, Norse Irish, fellow Normans, Bretons, Germans, Icelanders, Norsemen and Danes. One of the latter was Gunhild, sister of Sweyn, called Forkbeard, King of Denmark. Her husband, Pallig, recruited by Ethelred to protect his kingdom, had joined Viking raiders in the south-west.

Sweyn had rebelled against his father, Harald Bluetooth, who had died in battle during the rebellion. In Sweyn's youth he was captured by pirates, and the ladies of Denmark gave up their jewels to pay his ransom. In token of appreciation, Sweyn gave them the same rights to landed property as their male relatives.

But, to the English, Sweyn resembled a great shark cruising the seas, and in 994 the shark was seen in their inland waters. He thought to conquer all England and create an empire to rival that of the Germans, which was too strong to be overthrown. Rumours had come to him that some of Ethelred's council would be willing to have him as their king. He set sail with his Norse ally Olaf Tryggvason and about two thousand men and came up the river Thames to London. The Londoners, already showing their distinctive character and defiance of invaders, beat off the Vikings, who scattered and went through the surrounding shires as far as Hampshire, seizing the harvest and taking every horse they could find. Negotiations were held with Ethelred and his council who, following the advice of Sigeric, Archbishop of Canterbury, agreed to hand over sixteen thousand pounds. This was the second time the policy known as Danegeld was followed. Three years earlier the sum had been ten thousand pounds.

However, Ethelred had some reason to congratulate himself with reference to Olaf Tryggvason. He and Sweyn became bitter enemies following the marriage of Tryggvason to Thyra, sister of Sweyn. Tryggvason had been christened by a hermit on one of the Scilly Isles, during a pause while raiding Cornwall. He was now confirmed into the Church at Andover, and Ethelred was his godfather. Tryggvason declared that he would make himself King of Norway and bring Christ to that land.

A man of honour, Tryggvason fulfilled his pledge to leave England with his ships for good, but Sweyn took no part in the peacemaking. As soon as his money was handed over and the weather permitted, he took his fleet to the Isle of Man and stripped it of as much as he could as a consolation prize.

In the year 1000, Tryggvason, by now King Olaf of Norway, used much of his share of Ethelred's silver to build a mighty vessel, the *Long Dragon*. On a voyage to recover lands belonging to his wife, Thyra, King Olaf encountered Sweyn of Denmark at an island called Rugen, off the coast of Germany. The battle was fierce and Olaf was overwhelmed. Throwing away his weapons, he vaulted over the side of the ship into the sea, to be lost for ever, although it was said he was later seen as a pilgrim in Jerusalem.

While Sweyn of Denmark was away in the Baltic, settling his score with King Olaf, and the coasts of England were quiet, Ethelred took a resolve. He would no longer tolerate Viking settlers in his land. He would prove himself a warrior by going north to burn their homesteads and slay the people.

His astonished courtiers changed the theme of their flattery as they donned helmets and chainmail coats and took up small round shields bordered with iron and the single-edged short sword called the *seax* to accompany him. The militia, made up of peasants, marched behind. A fleet, hastily assembled with sailors grown rusty in the arts of defence, came out from Chester but missed meeting the army.

Ethelred and his troops killed, stole and burned among the Danes living in Strathclyde, an ancient British kingdom which stretched from the Clyde in the north down into Cumbria. The English ships then sailed to Man, which once again suffered plunder. Ethelred's men taught its Norse settlers that the English crown was not something vague and distant that could be safely disregarded.

The king returned south in triumph to his people's praise, but the experience was not one he wished to repeat. There were other ways to carry out ethnic cleansing. Like any modern dictator who draws up such a programme, he saw himself as the benefactor of his people – and this did not include the Danes.

Gunhild, sister of Sweyn, and her husband Pallig had sat at table with Ethelred and accepted money and lands from him. Before he set out on his northern campaign, the king ordered that Gunhild should be held hostage. Pallig was with Danes on their principal base, the Isle of Wight.

The Danes in the part of Mercia granted by Alfred to Guthrum had now been there for several generations. They had tilled and harvested land that had previously been barren. Their way of life and homesteads differed little from those of the Mercians. They had given up pagan worship, although some, as a kind of insurance, wore amulets in the shape of the hammer of Thor, rather than the cross of Christ. However, as Christians they came under the protective wing of the English king, as promised by Edgar.

But Ethelred, Edgar's son, likened the inhabitants of the Danelaw to the biblical 'tares' (weeds) among the wheat. He was resolved to drag them up by the roots.

It was not difficult to put secret orders around under cover of feasts with their harp and pipe music, recitations of performance poets and noise of laughter and banging of tables. On 13 November, the day dedicated to the French St Brice, when the harvests were in and the beasts slaughtered for winter food, messengers went out from the king with a royal order that Saxons and Mercians should kill the Danish settlers living among them. The king had been told that the Danes plotted to take over his kingdom. (Two years later, Ethelred himself admitted, apparently without shame, responsibility for the massacre.) In certain towns – notably the Five Boroughs, which had long been Danish, as well as York – it seems that, being outnumbered, the English could not fully carry out Ethelred's orders. But in Oxford the terrified Danes forced the doors of St Frideswide's church and broke in, seeking the protection of the Christian God from his Christian people. Those same people brought fire from the streets into the church, and the Danes died in the flames.

From the nearest abbeys of the stricken towns and homesteads came monks and priests to say prayers for the souls of those struck down without confession of their sins and preparation for death. Among the victims was Gunhild, the king's guest.

Emma and Ethelred produced only three children in fourteen years of marriage. Judging from the size of his first family, it would seem that Ethelred's first wife lived with him while Emma was usually at her own residence in Winchester. Perhaps, on the nights when they were together after the St Brice's Day Massacre, and the feasts were cleared away, the fires banked, the guards and watch-dogs settled for the night and the woven curtains and tapestries drawn, Emma turned on her husband and lashed him with her tongue, calling down all the furies and forces of revenge on him.

When the news was brought to Sweyn, he gathered together a

mighty fleet and his Norwegian and Swedish allies to wreak that revenge. Although he knew the day of the old gods Odin and Thor was done, he made sacrifices to them, calling on them to stand at his shoulder in his battles with the militia of the King of England.

Fear spread among the Saxons, particularly the people who lived along the coast, at news of the fleet's approach. Among the great and wealthy the fear was somewhat less. A country could be conquered only if its king was overthrown by his own people or slain in battle. So far, the people, remembering that Ethelred was the son of Edgar, called the Peaceful, were loyal, and his last intention was to venture on to the battlefield. Queen Emma was too valuable a counter in the diplomatic game to be harmed.

Sweyn came to Exeter, which had been twice taken by Danes and twice recovered in the days of Alfred. Here he met with an unexpected piece of good fortune. Hugh, the French reeve appointed to collect Emma's profits, was unconcerned as to whether Saxon or Dane was king in England – as maybe his mistress was, too. Either through carelessness or treachery he opened the city's gates, and the Danes swarmed in.

Sweyn's men went from Exeter into Wiltshire and burned Wilton and Salisbury, then returned to their ships. They often targeted the boroughs that had been fortified by Alfred and later attacked the land of the East Angles, which had once been an independent kingdom. There the Danes encountered effective opposition from the brave and loyal Earl Ulfcytel, married to Wulfhild, Ethelred's daughter. Although Norwich and Thetford were razed, Ulfcytel and his men struck fear into the invaders. He ordered their ships to be destroyed, but there were traitors among his own men, and the order was disobeyed.

Between the St Brice's Day Massacre and the death of Ethelred, England was nerve-wracked and apprehensive, drained of resources, although not officially at war and therefore unable to present a united front and a drive that would gain victory. The monks in their scriptoria, who recorded events for *The Anglo-Saxon Chronicles* from bulletins brought to their abbeys, tell of intermittent raids, attacks on towns, marches, failures of intelligence and confused commands. There were also times of respite, when it seemed that the enemy was in retreat but which turned out to be false hopes.

Throughout the turbulence the Saxons maintained the pattern of their existence as well as they could. Ethelred's court continued its removals around the country. Sometimes its wagons travelled along roads left by the Romans, or tracks beaten out by the feet of much earlier people, such as the Icknield Way, which runs from Norfolk to Wiltshire. The wagons passed fields where the crops had been ruined or were empty after herds had been driven off or which had never been used by man and in summer were crammed with the brilliance and beauty of wild flowers and loud with bees. On boundaries between estates, bodies and skeletons were often seen on gallows, not always left by Vikings but acting as witnesses of the king's justice against those who had committed theft, murder, arson and treason, crimes punishable by death.

Evidently Emma was required to undertake one of these journeys when she was near to giving birth. It was at Islip in Oxfordshire that her first child was born, and it should have been an occasion of much rejoicing, as the child was healthy and a boy. Ethelred gave him the name of Edward, that of his murdered brother, who should have been king of this unruly land.

Emma loved her children according to the man who fathered them and the stock from which he had been bred. The culture in which she lived did not encourage mother love among the ruling classes, but it did not extinguish the need for it, even among male children. It is safe to say that Edward utterly failed to win his mother's heart and that in due course Emma reaped a bitter harvest.

In 1005, a fearsome ally for the Saxons came in the form of natural disaster. The crops withered, while disease spread among farm animals. Because there was so little to steal, the Vikings took ship and left for Denmark. Ethelred also suffered the loss of his son Egbert this year.

By the eleventh century, Christian churches were calling their peoples to prayer across Europe as far east as Poland under its founder-ruler, Mieszko. Germany sought to convert Slavic peoples to the Church of Rome, but the rulers of the cities in the great wilderness of Russia with its Varangian river traders chose the eastern Church of Constantinople instead.

Almost every king, however much his behaviour clashed with Christian teachings, found it politic to respect churchmen and assist the Church with money and patronage. King Edgar, despite the scandals of his own life, had enabled Dunstan and Ethelwold to establish the Benedictine Rule in the abbeys of Wessex and East

Anglia. Earlier, the warrior Edward the Elder founded a nunnery at Romsey in Hampshire.

Ethelred was an exception to this piety. In his old age, Dunstan had retired to Canterbury, which adjoined the see of Rochester, also dating from Augustine's time. One of Ethelred's favourites advised him to lay claim to an estate belonging to Rochester. The bishop's men resisted the king, and Ethelred came with troops to besiege the town.

Its men stood out against the king, who let loose his soldiers to lay waste the villages and homesteads by the Medway. A messenger from the bishop came hotfoot to the school at Canterbury to beg for Dunstan's aid, but a letter commanding the king to mend his behaviour was ignored.

With a hundred pounds' weight in silver, the aged archbishop went to the bishop's residence, where the king was staying as an unwelcome guest. On receipt of the money, Ethelred agreed to leave Rochester and its bishop in peace.

In the year 1005, a new archbishop, almost as formidable as Dunstan, was appointed to Canterbury. His name was Alphege, and he had begun his career as a monk at Deerhurst in the Vale of Evesham. He was abbot of Bath Abbey in 973, when Edgar was crowned. His reputation as a holy man of great strictness spread among the citizens, who flocked to him, many becoming monks themselves. Some of these, however, lapsed and, instead of following monastic rules, held drunken feasts at midnight. From Bath, Alphege went to be Bishop of Winchester, and he escorted Olaf Tryggvason to his meeting with Ethelred and confirmation into the Church.

Like Dunstan, Alphege saw himself as the conscience of the king. But whereas Dunstan had dealt with boys and young men, Alphege was confronted by a man in his late thirties. Ethelred had already lived longer than all his five predecessors, and the archbishop's angry reminders of his coronation oath were like the buzzing of a fly on a hot summer's day. Ethelred's overall incompetence and genius for singling out the wrong people made it impossible to influence him for good.

The recovery of the kingdom after famine meant the return of the Danes. Soon after midsummer 1005 their fleet came across the North Sea and landed at Sandwich.

Ethelred sent out an order for every fighting man from Wessex and Mercia to come to the country's defence. But in autumn the Danes, well provisioned despite all attempts to thwart them, returned to their old base on the Isle of Wight. They landed on the Hampshire coast and marched along the Ridgeway, which is the part of the Icknield Way that crosses the Berkshire and North Wiltshire Downs. As they went they lit fires to mark their trail, and the flames shone under the bright stars of winter.

Their goal was a barrow at Cuckhamsley, where a West Saxon nobleman had been buried and where the court of the shire held its meetings. The local militia came out against them but were defeated. The Danes then turned back towards the coast, and from the walls of Winchester its citizens saw them pass, exulting over their booty.

Ethelred and Emma had left Wessex and travelled to Shropshire, that wild and beautiful part of Mercia still divided from Wales by the eighth-century earthwork and ditch called

Offa's Dyke, the longest defensive border in Europe. Here they held the midwinter feasts as well as they could, in the wake of famine and the ever-present fear.

Soon after this time a man called Edric Streona – the name means 'Grasper' – came to the forefront of Ethelred's council and court. The title of Earl of Mercia was revived for him, and he became part of Emma's extended family through marriage with her stepdaughter, Edith.

Most of the earls were of noble birth, some descended from the family of Alfred's brothers but not Edric Streona. However, this was no matter of a favourite with whom to share drinking and gaming and empty laughter. Edric was to be the king's chief general and councillor. He would rank higher than the growing sons of whom Ethelred was jealous and suspicious.

As for Emma the Queen, she was occupied not only with her own household but also with the bearing of another child, her daughter Goda, and overseeing the wet nurses provided for her.

Again the king and his council agreed to send money to the Danes. Again the clerks in charge of finance fixed the amount to be paid by each shire and appointed the officers who were to collect it. Again the cry went up, and the queen trembled for her revenues as a river of silver – thirty-six thousand pounds of it – was lost in the boundless ocean that was the Danes. This time the people were also obliged to give provisions out of their scanty stores, while imported goods were seized.

Among the traders of the Baltic, Norway, Denmark and the Swedish Varangians of Russia, coins with the inscription of Ethelred were becoming too common to cause comment. But peace was bought for some two years, and in the breathing space king and council drew up fresh laws for the defence of the land. Warships and armour were to be provided for a fleet that was to assemble after Easter every year, in numbers based on the variable unit of farming land called the hide.

In 1009, when the great fleet was ready, it gathered at Sandwich at Easter. Emma had reason to rejoice. At last the king was securing the land that was now her home and the monies that had been appointed for her.

But, as Ethelred was preparing to review the fleet, Brihtric, brother of Edric Streona, came and whispered to him that the commander of the Saxons of Sussex, Wulfnoth, was a traitor. Ethelred brought the accusation against Wulfnoth, who sent a signal along the line of ships drawn up on the Kentish shore. One after another was loosened from its anchorage until twenty were on the sea.

With his followers, Ethelred waited for the ships to return, but soon there came news that Wulfnoth's men had disembarked further south and were robbing the people there. So Ethelred gave Brihtric command of eighty ships of the fleet waiting at Sandwich.

Brihtric sailed away to the south without giving heed to the weather signs. A storm arose and threw the ships on shore, like so many whales. Wulfnoth and his men came down to the coast and set fire to the ships before they could put to sea again.

At Sandwich Ethelred abandoned his depleted fleet and turned back home with his chief councillors. The chronicler who recorded the event wrote of lack of luck and honour.

The remaining captains, with crews well armed and ready to do battle, ordered that their ships should put out to sea. They sailed by way of the Isle of Thanet, where the missionary Augustine had landed, and continued past the estuary of the Medway to the Thames and so to London.

Only the cold, clear water lapping on the Kentish shore was left after this example of gesture politics and mighty effort to raise money. The records were kept: in 1637 Ethelred's assessment for the tax was quoted in the trial of John Hampden for refusing to pay ship money. Another king, Charles I, had tried to impose this tax throughout the kingdom for the protection of his people and their trade but without the consent of Parliament. But no king had to submit to any parliament or endure its censure in the days of Ethelred, and his people lived as well as they could, defenceless against his whims, follies and spite. None could help them, least of all Emma the Queen, descended from a warrior caste and now a mature woman of some twenty-five years of age.

At Lammastide, the beginning of August, instead of the Saxon ships a Viking fleet was drawn up on the coast at Sandwich. It was led by two brothers, Thorkell and Hemming, of whom Thorkell was the mightiest and most renowned. They came to avenge another brother who had died in the St Brice's Day Massacre.

The men of Kent hastened to offer Thorkell and Hemming three thousand pounds, and the Danes returned to Wight from where they ranged far and wide over the counties of Wessex. They seized an estate in Wiltshire belonging to the nunnery of Winchester. To pay them off, the nuns were obliged to remove the gold, silver and gems from the tomb of St Edburga, daughter of Edward the Elder.

Ethelred called up the militia. With him went Edric Streona, Earl of the Mercians, and when the Danes continued unchecked, slipping like eels through the torn net of a fisherman, it was said that the counsel Streona gave the king was calculated not to confound but to assist the enemy.

Now, on the urging of Alphege, Archbishop of Canterbury, and Wulfstan, Archbishop of York, the people of England were exhorted to turn their thoughts to God and repent of their way of living. God, said the archbishops, far from being on their side, was judging them for their sins. The age of terrifying and pitiless churchmen, through whom the Church had made so much of its advance, was not over yet.

In response, Ethelred issued a law code directing that his subjects, many still thin from famine, should take only bread, herbs and water for three days in the week before the autumn festival of St Michael. They must give any uneaten food to the sick and poor and money to the Church and to beggars; they were to reverence relics, attend mass and pay any debts they owed. To mark this time of penitence, a coin was struck with the image of Christ on one side and the Holy Spirit in the form of a dove on the other. None the less, the Danish raids continued, and Oxford, where the settlers had been burned alive on St Brice's Day, was torched.

The Danish ships sailed to East Anglia, still held by Ulfcytel, Ethelred's son-in-law. To catch up with him and his men, the Danes had to march inland. The fight was fierce, but the Angles were defeated with the loss of many thanes. The horses of the

Danes moved swiftly over the land, even penetrating into the Fens, and with them rode the Horsemen of the Apocalypse: death, plague, famine and war. Farmers in their pastures were killed and their cattle driven away. Fires lit by the Danes were seen from afar over the flat land.

They burned Thetford and Cambridge, travelled through Oxfordshire and Buckinghamshire, burning as they went, and followed the river Ouse to Bedford. Such was the terror they spread that men from one shire would not help those from another. Late in November the Danes were burning Northampton. Having seized as much plunder as they could find, they crossed the Thames and by midwinter were back in Wessex.

It seemed to the writers of *The Anglo-Saxon Chronicles* in Peterborough – near the scenes of devastation although spared themselves – that when the Danes were in the east, the Saxons who should have been engaging them in battle were in the west, and when the Danes rode south, the Saxons went north.

Ethelred and his council offered the leaders money and provisions. The sum demanded was forty-eight thousand pounds. The Danes felt themselves entitled to continue with their raids while the king's officers again scoured the land for money.

Canterbury had stood firm this while, but in the autumn some of Thorkell's men laid siege to the town. Then a priest opened the gates to them, and the plunder, murder and burning began. Of their prisoners, the lesser folk were kept as slaves. The greater, including Archbishop Alphege, were imprisoned and payment demanded for their release.

The Danish fleet was waiting at Greenwich. The archbishop and some others were taken there when the Danes left Canterbury. They approached Edric Streona, Earl of the Mercians, who had come with other councillors to London for the raising of the full amount of the latest instalment of Danegeld. Now the Danes demanded three thousand pounds more for the release of Alphege. The archbishop himself refused to sanction this payment.

For seven months, throughout the winter until the Saturday after Easter, he was kept in bonds. Again and again he was told the money was ready; again and again he forbade its payment. It was meet that one man should die for the people.

During Easter, Alphege and his fellow Christians throughout the land meditated on the whips and scorns and sufferings of Jesus, whom they called the Lamb of God. Alphege had time to reflect on the likely nature of his own death. Edmund, King of the East Angles, was captured by Danes from the army that landed in 865. He was beaten with clubs, scourged with whips and pierced with spearheads. At last, as he called on Christ, his tormentors struck off his head. The place where he was buried, his head miraculously rejoined to his body, is called Bury St Edmunds. Alphege prepared himself for similar martyrdom. Through it he would be more worthy in the eyes of the Lord even than Dunstan, who had died in the arms of his monks.

Thorkell, the Christian Viking commander, offered to pay the archbishop's ransom but was refused. He knew from this that he had lost his authority and his life was at risk from his men. He therefore decided to defect to the Saxons at the next opportunity.

When Easter was past, wine from France unloaded at Greenwich was seized by the Danes and consumed at a feast at which an ox was roasted. Then they brought Alphege into their hall and again demanded money. The archbishop would not budge. One Dane struck him, then another; others took up the bones of the ox they had eaten and pelted him with them. They knocked him down with the largest bones and one, whom he had made a Christian, perhaps wishing to shorten Alphege's sufferings, crushed his skull with the blunt end of an axe.

Thus Alphege won his martyrdom, and his body lay all night among the smelly squalor of animal bones. With the morning came some churchmen and townspeople, who put the body in a cart and conveyed it upriver until they reached St Paul's Minster (on the site of which now stands Wren's St Paul's Cathedral). There they buried Alphege, and miracles were reported at his tomb.

In the months following, the Danes in London were racked by a dreadful illness, probably cholera caught from contaminated water, and some two thousand were struck down. A number who had taken part in Alphege's murder took ship and tried to escape the land where they had shed his blood, only to be drowned by shipwreck.

The payment of forty-eight thousand pounds by the English was at last complete, and more promises of peace were made. Thorkell went among his men, persuading as many as possible to join him in the service of the King of England. When the Danes had collected their booty and sailed away, forty-five ships were left with those who had listened to the arguments of Thorkell.

These men and ships were offered by Thorkell to Ethelred

some time near the end of the year 1012. He drove a hard bargain, but enough silver was left to pay the renegade Danes. Clothing of best English wool and leather was also provided, and Thorkell was given an estate in East Anglia. 'I swear', he said, 'to defend this country of England against all invaders.' New heart was put into Ethelred, Emma and the council. They would be safe in their beds now. Fire is best fought with fire.

News of Thorkell's defection was brought by the returning Danish ships to Sweyn Forkbeard in his palace in Jutland.

He considered it carefully. Now was the time to complete the work of vengeance for St Brice's Day. The English had been weakened, perhaps fatally, and they still had their hopeless king, Ethelred, rather than one of his fine brood of nearly adult sons.

Sweyn bought timber, pitch, sailcloth and ropes and set shipwrights to build a fleet for the final conquest of England. He discussed the project with his sons, for he did not hate his heirs as Ethelred did his own. The younger son, Knutr, known to the Saxons as Cnut (and later as Canute), was some nineteen years old. He showed more interest in the affairs of England than his brother Harold, and Sweyn resolved to take him along.

The Danish fleet was decorated with gilded and silver figures of men, lions, dragons, bulls and dolphins, with the wind vanes in the form of birds, and the sides of the ships were brightly painted, gilded and silvered. The glittering and intimidating splendour appeared off Sandwich in the summer days of 1013. Here it waited for a few ships that had fallen behind. Then Sweyn turned northward and, as he went, news of his coming spread through those parts of England where the remaining Danish people lived, until he came to the Humber Estuary, into which flows the river Trent. There he disembarked at the town of Gainsborough, where Uhtred, Earl of Northumbria – married to Ethelred's daughter Elgiva – and the leading Danish settlers came to him, laid down their arms and gave him fresh horses and provisions.

Like a dark stain spreading across a cloth, the Danes marched and rode south. Once across Watling Street Sweyn let his men loose. Oxford and royal Winchester fell. In Oxford Sweyn paused to give one of his commanders pagan burial with his horse, stirrups and spurs. He then turned towards London, where Ethelred was waiting with Thorkell's ships at Greenwich – those ships for which he had paid so high a price and which had been no more use against Sweyn than splintered wrecks.

The Londoners garrisoned the city and succeeded in holding out against the Danes. They were helped because some of Sweyn's men, not finding a bridge, plunged into the river in their eagerness to cross and many were drowned. Sweyn then drew back his army and ordered it to march west to Bath, to complete the subjugation of Wessex. Thorkell offered Ethelred living space on his ships, but this was scarcely fit for Emma the Queen and her three children, Edward, Goda and Alfred.

Ethelred ordered Emma to go with Goda to Normandy and her brother's protection, to be joined later by the two boys. Edward had been studying with the monks of Ely, among the pleasant gardens and orchards that had been planted there.

The Abbot of Peterborough accompanied the queen. Whether

it was his presence, or because Ethelred had kept Emma in the background so that no blame for his ill deeds fell on her, or simply because the company was not seen and stopped in their flight, they made the coast in safety and went aboard a suitable boat for Normandy. Returning through the windblown hours by the route she had travelled as a bride, Emma, with the abbot and Goda, at last came to harbour and told the men who gathered to unload the ship that she was sister to their duke.

Emma was back in her own country with the relations of her blood and language who addressed her by her own name. Away from the eye of the storm she was able to take stock of her position and its ambiguities. She was no longer a Norman noblewoman, and while Ethelred lived she could not revert to her origins. She had been crowned Queen of England, and her image was as fixed as that of a chessboard piece. Moreover, besides being her home, England was the source of her revenues and remaining in Normandy would mean giving up her wealth. Whatever the humiliations heaped on her by Ethelred, she must hope for his restoration or at least that of his line.

Meanwhile, she must endure another humiliation as the object of the commiserations and hospitality of her brother Richard and Judith, his wife. Their hospitality was extended to her sons, who soon arrived safely. Their half-brothers stayed in England.

Ethelred had lived and reigned long – longer, it was to prove, than most kings in English history. If his time came soon, Emma would still be queen and able to bear children to a new and better husband. In due course she might even marry one of her older stepsons. This would have echoed the story of Judith, a young

Frankish princess who had been married to Ethelwulf, King of Wessex, when he had a grown-up family which included the future King Alfred. On Ethelwulf's death in 858, Ethelbald, one of Alfred's brothers, married his stepmother.

But any idea of replicating this historical event was nipped in the bud by another arrival in Normandy – that of Ethelred himself.

In Bath, old men and women spoke of the coronation of Edgar they had witnessed as children. What a day of celebration that had been. Now, in the reign of Edgar's younger son, they must watch as a grim Danish warrior, with eyes that could make even Vikings quail, rode into their city. With him came a rowdy company, and the noblemen of the West Country acknowledged his authority over them.

Sweyn then set out for Gainsborough, where his ships were waiting under the command of Canute. As he went, people came out from their boroughs or villages to salute him. Word came to London that Sweyn of Denmark was King of England and the leaders of the Londoners prepared to swear allegiance to him. Thorkell's interest in Ethelred was finished, except for the money the king still owed him for his help and loyalty to England.

There was nothing for the king to do but quit his kingdom. When the Danes came through the gates in London Wall, Ethelred was stealing towards the south coast and Wight, where he was received by Danes loyal to Thorkell. Then, in the month of January, he crossed to Normandy, and Emma received him with the best grace she could.

There was an outcry from the Church at Ethelred's departure.

According to Archbishop Wulfstan, the king was still Christ's representative, and all who deserted him put their own souls in jeopardy.

On 3 February 1014, death came to a king; not Ethelred but Sweyn Forkbeard, King of Denmark and England. He died at Gainsborough. Full of bloody and fearful deeds though his life had been, it was reported that on his deathbed he commended the Church to his son Canute. A rumour spread that his death, so near the hour of victory, was the vengeance of St Edmund, that king slain by the Danes. King Sweyn's body was preserved and laid in a grave at York.

The men of the fleet in the Trent hailed Canute as their king, and he was proclaimed as such by leading men in Southampton. From across the sea a cry came to Ethelred and Emma and the rest of the English in Normandy. Messages were brought to the king from the councillors he had left behind. In the face of rule by foreigners, they declared, remembering Alfred and Edgar: 'No lord is dearer to us than our lord by birth.' Then, the all-important qualification: 'If he would rule us better than before.'

The Norman lords laughed, their eyes hard as the iron of their helmets and chainmail.

There was a place for his children in Normandy, Ethelred knew, but not for him. When the embassy arrived from England to discuss his return, the king's scribe prepared a letter in which the king spoke to his subjects as equals. He sent greetings and the promise that he would indeed be a better lord to them. Their grievances would be dealt with and all treachery forgiven. The

Saxon embassy agreed these terms and declared there would be no Danish kings in England.

It was arranged that the younger children would stay at the Norman court while Edward sailed to England with the embassy. (He was evidently a forward boy for his age.) The news was told to a certain high-born Norseman called Olaf Haraldsson, a great warrior who had fought in the Baltic lands, in France and Spain and also in East Anglia and at Canterbury, both times against the English. Now he was in the service of Duke Richard while waiting to return to Norway to seize the throne. Seeing Ethelred as a possible ally, he offered his ships as an escort for the voyage to England. Ethelred took up Olaf's offer, and he and Emma returned during Lent. The country's militia came to Ethelred to prepare to drive Sweyn's heir, Canute, back to Denmark.

At some time between his arrival in England with his father and Sweyn's death, Canute, that strange contradiction of merciless Viking and servant of the Church, had fallen in love and remained so for the rest of his life. The object of his love was Elgiva, called Elgiva of Northampton, who had been unprotected since her father, a Northumbrian earl, was executed in 1006 by Ethelred, who also blinded her two brothers. Elgiva became Canute's handfast wife.

While gathering men and horses for a final battle over the English, Canute heard that Ethelred was on the road at the head of an army. The resurgence of loyalty told him the people were not ready to accept a Dane as king, particularly the men of Lindsey, the ancient Anglian kingdom that is part of Lincolnshire. Canute turned tail and left his allies to confront Ethelred's army. At

Sandwich he cut off the hands, ears and noses of the hostages his father had taken.

The few left in authority acknowledged Ethelred's restored kingship, and he remembered his debt to the men of the fleet waiting in the Thames. His first order to his newly formed council was to raise another twenty-one thousand pounds and send them to Thorkell the Dane.

There was peace in England, peace of an uneasy, unreal kind. Everywhere there were shortages – not only of coin but also goods to be exchanged where coin was lacking. The farmers worked to build up their depleted stocks and resow the ravaged fields.

The Danes were gone, but the sea that had brought them to England turned hostile, flooding many stretches of the English shores in September 1014. Rivers swelled and spilled over fields, cattle and sheep were drowned, and many of the country people, after clinging to the roof beams of their homes, were swept into the roaring waters.

Emma returned to her Winchester home, Godbegot. At court, life resumed some semblance of normality. The king attempted to disregard the reproaches directed at him and his subjects by Wulfstan. The Archbishop of York thundered denunciations of carelessness in religious matters and also referred to the unavenged murder of King Edward the Martyr.

The younger Edward went back to Normandy, where he ceased to feel himself a Saxon. If any bond had begun to form between him and his mother, it was terminated.

At the feasts the men in favour with the king were again seen whispering into his ear under cover of the noise of the hall. Still prominent among these was Edric Streona. He had a private quarrel with two Danish lords called Siferth and Morcar, who had taken English territory. Streona asked them to meet him at Oxford when the council assembled there. They brought with them Aldgyth, the wife of Siferth. Edmund, son of the king, was seized with love for her. Following the deaths of his brothers, Athelstan and Egbert, this Edmund was first in line for succession to the throne. He, above all others, was the one whom those with true hearts wished to see as king in place of his father. He became known as Ironside.

Streona received his guests with every sign of friendship. That night, hired assassins did their work with Siferth and Morcar, although Aldgyth was not touched.

Ethelred acted quickly to prevent any further breach of hospitality. An armed guard took Aldgyth to the abbey of Malmesbury in Wiltshire, while the king declared the estates of both Siferth and Morcar to be forfeit.

Ironside came to his father and asked to be given Aldgyth in marriage. Ethelred refused. The woman his son desired was a widow, as Ethelred's own mother had been – Elfrida, who by conspiracy of murder had given him this burden of England that he could not rule.

Within a few weeks there was a summons at the doors of the abbey of Malmesbury. A young man with the air of a bridegroom, who said he was Edmund, the king's son, asked to see Aldgyth. The wooing was swift. A priest was called and the marriage ceremony performed. Then Ironside marched to the Five Boroughs of the Danelaw and claimed Siferth's forfeit property. Those who had suffered under Ethelred's recent invasion and remembered the St Brice's Day Massacre rallied to him.

Streona swore an oath to Ethelred that he would not rest until he had brought Ironside back to obedience to his father. Ethelred himself was unable to go in pursuit of his son because of the onset of serious illness.

Thorkell the Dane, with Ethelred's twenty-one thousand pounds on board, left the Thames with nine warships and sailed north to his natural allegiance. Canute made him welcome and confided his plans for England to him. To carry them out, he entered into alliance with Earl Eric of Norway, who had joined with Sweyn in the defeat of Olaf Tryggvason in 1000. He was a great and renowned warrior.

Canute was less concerned with vengeance than his father had been. St Brice's Day belonged to the previous generation. Instead, Canute looked to kingship in England, with Elgiva of Northampton at his side.

While waiting for the best time to invade, he attended to family matters. With his elder brother Harold, now King of Denmark, he travelled to Poland to fetch their mother. Her identity is subject to conjecture: she may have been the daughter of Mieszko of Poland, but another possibility is that she was Sigrid, the pagan widow of Eric, King of Sweden.

In the meantime, an English lady had been ordering a ship to be prepared for a voyage to Denmark. When it was ready, she had the body of Sweyn Forkbeard disinterred and covered with palls and took it on board the ship with her. On their return from

Poland, Sweyn's sons received a message from this lady to the effect that their father's body was awaiting burial in the monastery at Roskilde that Sweyn had built. Canute and Harold hastened to receive the body and gave it a royal funeral.

Nothing more is known of this lady or her motives. It sounds as though Sweyn, as well as Canute, may have contracted a hand-fast marriage in England.

Canute assembled a fleet of some two hundred ships, hung with shields of many designs and ornamented with gold and silver figures of men and beasts. It was said that there were no slaves among his men, nor anyone who had once been a slave, nor anyone low-born or aged. They came up the English Channel in September 1015, before the autumn gales blew up.

It may well be that the news of their coming, when brought to the queen, left her unmoved. To one man at least, Edric Streona, the sight was even pleasing. The line of Alfred was withering away; what green shoots remained could easily be cut down. He who wished to prosper and hold power should join the young Danish leader. And he who brought with him the earldom of Mercia and its fighting men would be set little lower than the king when the Danish conquest was complete. With this in mind, Streona persuaded the crews of forty of Ethelred's ships to accompany him when he came to Canute.

The Danish fleet anchored in Poole harbour, and by midwinter Canute had taken Wessex. Ironside attempted to raise an army in Mercia, including the Danelaw, where he had assumed authority after taking possession of Siferth's property. But Ethelred was still king, and the Mercians demanded his presence, together with the

London militia, their troops being insufficient in number to withstand the Danes.

Spurred on by the wish to capture and punish Streona, the false favourite in whom he had put so much trust, Ethelred came to Ironside with a battalion of warriors from Wessex. But the air was full of whispers, charges and counter-charges. Without Streona by his side, Ethelred did not know who or what to believe. Here in Mercia he was on unfamiliar ground. London was the only place where he felt safe. He gathered an escort and hurried off.

Uhtred, Earl of Northumbria, Ironside's brother-in-law, agreed to destroy the enemy's sources of supply in Cheshire, Shropshire and Staffordshire. Ironside had taken all his men on this campaign, and Canute, with Streona and the Norse Earl Eric, marched northwards along the Great North Road where the Roman legions had passed.

Earl Uhtred came to the Midlands from his own earldom, but at the Danish camp his heart failed him and he went to Canute to make his surrender. It did him little good, for assassins hiding behind the tapestries of the hall slew him at the instigation of the Yorkshireman Thurbrand, the earl's enemy. This brought about one of the worst and longest lasting of the blood feuds the kings had long tried to contain.

Canute promised Northumbria to Earl Eric and turned back to Wessex. Word of his movements came to Ironside, who ordered a march to London. Along his route, men who still hoped to see the Dane defeated joined his train, and so they entered London.

To Ethelred II, most undeserving of English kings, whose reign has no redeeming feature (unlike those of John, Henry VIII, even Richard III), was granted the boon of dying in his bed at a relatively late age. By touching his head, hands and feet with holy oil and praying for the entry of his soul into Paradise, the priests wiped out even his worst sins: lies, treachery, cruelty and oppression, and the message sent by night for the slaying of his Danish subjects.

If Emma stood at Ethelred's deathbed and wondered if he would come into the presence of his God, she had only to remember that the Church had provided him with two saints for kindred, Edward the Martyr and Edith, daughter of Edgar and Wulfrid. They had died long ago, for Ethelred was now forty-eight. But they would doubtless be waiting at the throne of the heavenly grace to intercede for him.

Ethelred died on 23 April in the year 1016. Because he had been crowned king, his body was taken to St Paul's which, after a fire, had been rebuilt in stone. This church was also burned down, and its successor was later destroyed in the Great Fire of London of 1666. Perhaps a few bones of Ethelred the Unready remain deep in the earth, below the tombs and memorials to Nelson and Wellington, Trafalgar and Waterloo.

EDMUND IRONSIDE

The earls and thanes of England met to choose who, Saxon prince or Danish invader, should be their sovereign lord. The question needed to be settled quickly, before the land fell into the worst anarchy of the Viking Age.

The leading men of London and those who had come into the city with Edmund Ironside proclaimed him as king. Somewhere a crown was found or hastily hammered out by a smith. Lyfing, Archbishop of Canterbury, setting it on Ironside's head, repeated as much of the coronation ceremony as he could from memory.

Some two weeks later a message came that in Southampton the rest of the council, with the bishops and abbots of Wessex, had confirmed the proclamation of Canute as king, dismissing the claim of the Saxon line. Canute swore loyalty to them in return. Thus there was no kingdom for Ironside except within the walls of London.

The mood of the people who had cried for Ethelred to return from Normandy had changed, as a weathervane swings in the wind. This Canute was a young man, less filled with a thirst for vengeance than his father had been. The Church believed it would be safe under his rule. Why, therefore, should it not welcome the Danes and seek to live with them in peace and trust, as in the days of Edgar?

Ironside remained in London, debating with his supporters. Emma the Queen was under his protection. The division between Saxons and Danes was too sharp for her to do anything other than stand with her family by marriage.

Ironside left London to rally the western men. But Canute came first to Greenwich, then made a canal along the south bank of the Thames and took his ships to the west of the great log bridge that defended the city. The Danes then built a line of earthworks outside London's walls. Among Canute's men was probably Olaf Haraldsson, the Norseman Ethelred had known in Normandy. Canute and Olaf were to play very different parts in each other's lives later.

Emma, under siege with the Londoners, waited to hear that the question of kingship had been settled one way or the other. The news of the siege reached the Continent, and its outcome was eagerly awaited. A German chronicler saw Emma as attempting to bring about peace between the opponents. Verses were later sung at Canute's court of how she watched the fighting and waited for news of Canute's victory.

Certainly, her experiences as Ethelred's wife had not given her reason to feel that her future happiness and safety lay with the Saxons. The stepson whom she may have loved and hoped to marry had been bewitched by another woman. She had Danish blood. If good fortune was on the side of the Danes, it might be to her advantage.

The Danes' time, however, had not yet come. In the west, many Britons joined the Saxons who came to hail Ironside as their king. Once another chieftain had stood in Cornwall against earlier

Saxons, and in after years he was called King Arthur. But Ironside, although crowned king, was unsure of the loyalty of his own people, and the militia he raised grew more and more ragged, carrying stones and slings instead of spears and inlaid swords. With Ironside went his wife, Aldgyth.

Leaving his men at the ramparts outside the walls of London, Canute travelled west in search of Ironside. Men from Wessex were with his troops, also the dark shadow that was Edric Streona, Earl of Mercia. At Sherston in Wiltshire, Ironside fought hand to hand in the front line. He had previously gained an advantage at Selwood in Somerset, but at Sherston Streona held up a hacked-off head, crying that it was that of Ironside. Then the English prince, ascending a mound, took off his helmet and showed the words, like so many of Streona's, to be a lie.

In the summer twilight the fighting ceased and the armies drew back from each other, lit their fires and settled down for the short night. Before light came in the east, Canute's soldiers were roused and prepared to march. The Saxons, waking under the dawn sky, heard the sound of retreating feet along the road to London.

Ironside gathered his men together and followed Canute's army until they found the Danes in their encampment on the north bank of the Thames. The Saxons, suddenly descending, put them to flight. The Danes took to their ships, and two days later Ironside crossed the river at Brentford. In a battle on the south bank of the Thames the English were the victors, but many were drowned in an attempt to seize loot. Judging London to be secured, Ironside took his remnant into Wessex and sent messengers to rally every young man they found to take up arms in the cause of their Saxon king.

Emma in London heard the sounds of men beyond the city walls as the Danes resumed the siege of Ironside's kingdom. But the land they had plundered was unable to provide the supplies they needed, so Canute took his fleet out of the Thames and sailed to East Anglia and Mercia. They arrived as grain and fruits were ripening, and herds of horses, cattle and sheep were theirs for the taking.

The fleet returned to the Medway, but Ironside, who had collected fresh troops from all over Wessex, drove the Danes into the island of Sheppey. It seemed as though victory would at last be his. Edric Streona saluted him as king. Ironside, because of the numbers of men under the turncoat's command, took him into his company.

He pursued the Danes in a raid across Essex, and they met in battle at a low hill at Ashingdon, between the rivers Thames and Crouch. Soon there was a swirling like water among the Saxon troops. Streona had withdrawn the men he had brought from the borders of Wales.

Relics had been brought from Ely in order to bring the Saxons luck, but many of their noblemen were killed in the Battle of Ashingdon, including Ulfcytel, Earl of East Anglia, husband of Wulfhild, Ethelred's daughter. But Ironside escaped into Gloucestershire, and word came to Canute that his rival, still undefeated in spirit, was yet again seeking reinforcements to drive the Danes from England. Because of his ability to draw men to him, it seemed best to compromise.

Canute spoke to his councillors and the Saxons who had joined him, including Edric Streona. An embassy was sent to Ironside, who late in the autumn came to Deerhurst in the Vale of Evesham. The scent of hay and fallen leaves was in the air, rather than blood, carrion and fear. As the two leaders met, men remarked on how mighty a man Ironside was and how mean the Dane seemed in his presence.

A pact was made between them, a pledge of friendship and agreement of payment for the Danish army. England was divided between the two. Canute was to rule all the country north of the Thames. Edmund Ironside was given Wessex. The question 'What of the queen?' was not asked.

The monks in the abbeys offered thanks for the peace treaty and prayed as heartily for Canute as for Ironside. There must always be a king in England, and it mattered little to the people whether he was Saxon or Dane when they were required to pay out yet more silver, this time to the enemy army that had ruined so much of their country. The injustice was felt still more by the Londoners, because they had to pay a separate sum for the maintenance not only of the soldiers but also the Danish ships that had been moored in the Thames until the spring.

On 30 November 1016, the feast day of St Andrew, Edmund, called Ironside, last King of Wessex, met his *wyrd*. He was twenty-three years old. How he died has been much debated. For long it was thought he was murdered by an agent of Canute or the traitor Edric Streona. Modern scholars, however, believe it is more likely to have been through illness or accident.

According to *The Anglo-Saxon Chronicles*, Ironside was buried with Edgar at Glastonbury, the site of Avalon, the land of Morgan le Fay the enchantress, Ogier the Dane and Arthur the King. Years later, Canute, then nearing middle age, came to Glastonbury and laid a pall worked in blues, greens and gold on Ironside's tomb. However, a twelfth-century inscription referring to 'Edmund son of King Ethelred' on a Purbeck marble slab in Winchester Cathedral could mean that this was the burial place of Edmund Ironside, and his bones may lie in the cathedral's mortuary chests.

CANUTE THE KING

Early in 1017, Canute, King of England by conquest but not yet crowned, was in London, discussing a matter of great moment with leading churchmen. The matter, the marriage of the king, was the same that had been discussed fifteen years before by Ethelred and his council. Even the proposed bride was the same. This time, however, Emma was far from the young girl who had waited while the Saxon embassy to Rouen asked her brother Richard for her hand. She was a woman hardened by years of unhappy marriage in frightening and unsafe times but to some extent in control of her own destiny.

She could have made several moves. No doubt there were men willing to help her take refuge in Normandy, as she had done once before. One of the surviving Saxon earls might have risked the wrath of the king and married her, as Edmund Ironside had married the widowed Aldgyth. With Ironside dead, the Saxon line seemed at an end. This was not something to cause Emma, queen and outsider, any regret. She had known no reign but Ethelred's. Alfred had died long ago, and the tales of England as it had been in his days were like the stories of poets. Canute the Dane, a man of her mother's blood, would begin a new line, and who more fit to give him children than one who had already been crowned and sanctified queen? It was convenient, although incidental, that she had been brought up to speak Danish.

She could, of course, have taken the approved route for the widowed or discarded wives of Saxon kings and entered the Church. This would have meant a complete change of lifestyle. Thanks to the reforms of Dunstan and Ethelwold, nuns lived a relatively strict and frugal life. Even in Ethelred's straitened times, Emma had known luxury and privilege. With warfare over, these would be increased.

What was good for her, however, was less so for her children, who were also the children of Ethelred. They were still in Normandy, and there they must remain for their own safety. Fortune might yet restore them to her side, but if it did not the duke would no doubt provide for their education, give Edward and Alfred promotion and arrange a fitting marriage for Goda in due course. They would call no other woman by the name of mother.

If the figure of Canute and the prospect of marriage to him grew daily brighter in Emma's imagination, his reason for agreeing to marry Ethelred's widow was the renewal of the link with Normandy that she represented. Not only would it block any future claim to England by Ethelred's youngest sons, but it meant the continuation of a foothold on the Continent, nearly a century after King Athelstan had traded his sisters for French and German friendship. Edgar's imperialistic pretensions had been more imaginary than real, not extending beyond his grand coronation at Bath. And under Ethelred the kingdom had thought of survival rather than expansion.

Now all that was over. For a start, Canute brought with him an alliance with Denmark, of which his brother was king. And there was no reason why his new realm with its fair southern land, mild and green, wealthy in grain harvests and wool, should not continue to look still further south. He was willing to marry the Flower of Normandy, but it had to be on his own terms.

He conveyed as much to the churchmen conducting the betrothal negotiations. They had started these knowing they must make the best of a bad job. The long years of struggle against Vikings had ended with a Viking king in England. But Canute assured them that he would give every support to their task of reasserting the Church's authority over those who had come to feel that God had left them to the devils of the sea. He intended to enter the company of Christian kings. As a way of doing this, he had shown reverence for two Saxon martyrs. Besides expressing penitence for the murder of Archbishop Alphege, he had declared his wish to establish a saint's day for the young King Edward, a convenient reminder that Ethelred's accession had been stained with blood.

This was all admirable, but there were two drawbacks to committing himself to Christian marriage with Emma. The first was that the Church frowned on marriages to widows. Archbishop Dunstan had condemned Edgar to go uncrowned for seven years because he had put aside his wife for the widow Elfrida. But Elfrida had not brought with her an alliance with a European power. Emma's widowhood could be overlooked. The second drawback was more serious. Canute, young as he was – younger by about ten years than the queen – was married already.

The Northumbrian lady Elgiva had tended and encouraged

him in the days of uncertainty when the kingship of England had danced before his eyes like lights in a marsh. She had borne him three children. She and they must be out of sight before Canute's offer of marriage could be brought to Emma the Queen.

The churchmen put this to the king, little doubting his consent. His reply was unexpected. There was to be no banishment for Elgiva. He refused to enter into any discussion of the question. Emma would be his wife according to the Church, but Elgiva had a claim on his heart, otherwise as cold as the winters of the North. It is not known if Emma had already heard gossip of Elgiva's existence or whether a red-faced churchman enlightened her. The news, however it came, was enough to strike her into the semblance of a queen carved from ivory. The security she believed Canute would give her – and which she had never known before – was threatened by another, younger woman, who seemed like a mocking copy of herself. Her name was the same as that which the English had given Emma, but it was this Elgiva's true name. Some might say that her marriage, although handfast, was also the true one. Even her children were a reminder of Emma's own – two boys and a girl.

The stakes were high; marriage with a man of lower degree or returning to Normandy a second time would be as humiliating as accepting another woman in her husband's life. Emma put aside any hopes she may have had of love and made a winning calculation by looking to the future. At least the Englishwoman's sons should not prevail.

She told the go-between that she would marry Canute if he promised that no son of any wife but her should succeed to his

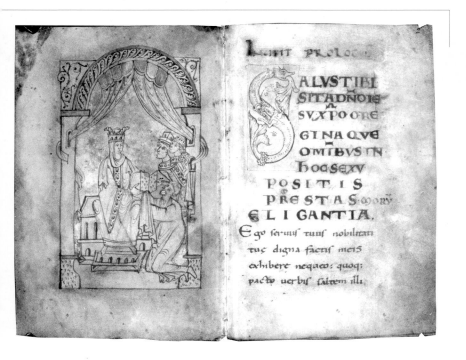

The frontispiece and dedication of the presentation copy of Emma's encomium. The text calls on Christ to preserve 'the admirable and excellent' Emma and the writer regrets his 'unworthiness'. The illustration is unusual for its time in having a secular theme, although there is a faint echo of the Magi in the group around Emma.

This page and the following two pages show illustrations from the manuscript of a verse life of Edward the Confessor written in the thirteenth century. Sweyn and his Danes are on the left, creating general mayhem; on the right, Emma and her sons Edward and Alfred are escorted on their flight to Normandy.

Canute and Edmund Ironside fighting for the English crown (left of picture) and then making peace (centre right); the right side of the manuscript shows its version of Edmund's death.

The curious episode of Edward finding a thief in his treasury and warning him to make his escape.

Opposite: One of the mortuary chests in Winchester Cathedral and the bones it contains. There are various theories concerning the identities of these skeletal remain, but it is likely that the remains of Emma and Canute are among them. Others here a Egbert and Ethelwulf – grandfather and father of Alfred the Great – and King Edred. Alfred himself was probably buried at the New Minster, but his bones do not seem to in the cathedral. The body of William Rufus, second of the Norman kings and Emma's kinsman, was brought to Winchester in 1100 and buried beneath the tower of Walkelin's new cathedral. At some point Rufus's bones joined those from the Saxon burial ground.

The shrine of Edward the Confessor as it appears today in
Westminster Abbey. Since the Dissolution of the Monasteries,
Edward's bones have lain in an unknown and unmarked grave
in the Abbey. However, his coffin was returned to the shrine
by Mary I in 1557, and Edith seems to have been left undisturbed.

Edward's seal, attached to a writ in Old English, is a reminder
of his political power, which contributed to the ascendancy
of London as England's capital city.

The Great East Window of York Minster showing Edward the Confessor holding his ring (left) and William the Conqueror. William, as depicted here by the glazier John Thornton in the early fifteenth century, is quite unlike the figure on the Bayeux Tapestry.

Francis Spear's modern stained-glass panel in St Alfege's Church, Greenwich. The martyr also appears in the church's east window.

A silver arm ring found in Gainsborough, Lincolnshire. Lincolnshire was part of the region of England known as the Danelaw. (City and County Museum, Lincoln)

A spearhead of Scandinavian pattern from Chippenham, Wiltshire, where the Danes were encamped in 878, the year of Alfred's victory at nearby Edington. (Wiltshire Heritage Museum, Devizes)

A coin of Ethelred the Unready from Winchester. (Winchester Museums Service)

throne. The condition did not seem unreasonable to Canute. What happened with his sons would be after he had entered the heaven the churchmen seemed ready to promise him. He gave his assent.

Besides Emma's sons, there were two other young boys whom Canute wished to see permanently banished or, better still, put to death – like Edwy, the only surviving son of Ethelred's first marriage, who had been murdered on his orders. Saxons loyal to the memory of Ironside warned his widow, Aldgyth, to flee with her two sons far beyond the shores of England. Ironside had given these boys the royal names of Edmund and Edward.

The trials of their journey must have been almost beyond imagining. Once in Europe, they travelled east, using traders' routes and great rivers, obtaining food from villages and fishermen as they went. They crossed the German Empire and the mountains of Austria, going still further east until they reached the Hungarian plain, which had been invaded more than a century before by savage Magyar tribes. In the ninth century these tribes lived on the steppes west of the lower Don. They were nomadic horsemen who plundered from and enslaved their neighbours. Later they migrated across the Carpathian mountains and conquered more territory, where they continued their way of life or fought as mercenaries for the European states. But eventually they were defeated by the Germans, and, in 975, their chief, Geza, became a Christian.

In 1017, Hungary, the land of the Magyars, was ruled by Geza's son Istvan, called Stephen in the West, who had been crowned by the Pope in the year 1000. This king received the Saxon asylum seekers, cast the cloak of his protection over them and gave them places of honour at his court. Here they were out of Canute's reach, but it was not until more than twenty years after his death that one of them dared to appear in England again.

At a meeting of the English Council it was declared that the Saxons had no right to the throne. But at another meeting Canute made an oath of friendship to the people, which would be confirmed by his marriage with their queen. Among other laws, one was passed enabling a widow to marry again a year and a day after her first husband's death and with her consent. It should not be said that he was treating Emma as the spoils of war.

At last she was called to her July marriage. She rode out of London, leaving behind the ramparts and canal Canute had constructed during his struggle with Ironside and the river Thames, along which armed bodies had floated. Now merchant ships from across the Channel and also from the Vikings' own Baltic Sea were anchoring at its quays again.

Emma travelled until she reached the chalk downs of the south, where those who had lived in the land before the Romans came lay beneath grassy mounds with bronze and iron swords and ornaments of twisted gold. Soon she was in Winchester, where the surprising news of her return as Canute's queen was being broadcast throughout the city.

In Godbegot, her home, repairs were carried out, floors swept and those articles that had disappeared during her absence replaced. Again it would be a habitation fit for a queen to live in and receive guests, including her husband the king. All that was lacking were the voices of children, a lack that would surely soon be made up by the birth of an heir to the Danish line, stronger than the Saxons, derived from Vikings and destined to restore the prosperity of Edgar's time.

Such a guarantee was necessary for a queen who came without the dowry of silk, gold, silver and attendants that had been sent with her when she arrived for her first marriage at the height of her beauty.

On the wedding and coronation day (probably the same), Canute repeated the oath that Edgar had made to Dunstan at his crowning:

I swear the Church of God and all Christian people shall enjoy
> true peace for ever.
I swear to forbid all wrong and robbery to all degrees.
I swear to command justice and mercy in all judgements.

Then the familiar feel of the rounded rim of a crown on Emma's head. She was again queen of the English, but the ceremony that made her part of the new rule over England was, for all the chantings of the mass, a compromise wrung from double-dealing churchmen. At the wedding feast, the usual references to the groom's manhood and the bride's virginity would have been replaced by covert speculation as to whether Canute's first Elgiva might be found in possession of the bridal bed.

When news of the marriage reached Normandy, many people were puzzled and disapproving. A Latin poem called *Semiramis* was written, satirizing the union as one between a harlot queen and a bull.

Emma's three children knew their mother had deserted them. Edward, now in his teens and already dedicated to chastity, was old enough to understand the significance of the grins and sniggers of his retainers as they spoke of the marriage. A Viking had bedded his mother – and she was willing.

Canute made several symbolic gestures to impress the legitimacy of Danish rule upon England. He commissioned a great stone frieze illustrating legends recognized in both Wessex and Denmark. It was set up in the Old Minster, although little of it now remains. He also dedicated 18 March to Edward the Martyr, this being the date of the assassination at Corfe.

The Danish king followed Saxon tradition by establishing the seat of his government at Winchester. In a balcony on the first floor of the spire of the Old Minster, built when Alphege was bishop, a throne was placed for the king to look down into the nave during the crown-wearing ceremony. This was held every few years for the leading men of the land to see the king in all his regalia and be reminded of his power over them.

Canute had a royal residence in what is now Westminster, but London was regarded as a mere mercantile city compared with Winchester.

Although Winchester was the official home of the king and the woman all recognized as his lawful wife, Canute also had a home at what is now the pretty village of Old Bosham on a creek of the Sussex shore. It was there that he visited Elgiva of Northampton and their little daughter.

He was with Emma often enough for the birth of a son, an

occasion of great joy, altogether unlike the birth of Edward in the wake of his six half-brothers. Now the Saxons, including Emma's older sons, were finally excluded from the vision of the new Danish-ruled England. And, no less important to her, Elgiva's sons Sweyn and Harold were eclipsed by the new baby, Hardecanute.

Canute divided England into its four traditional regions and set earls over three of them. East Anglia was given to Thorkell and Eric of Norway confirmed as Earl of Northumbria. Canute himself kept Wessex. Edric Streona retained Mercia for a while but was soon accused of treason and executed by beheading.

The year after the coronation, some thirty Viking ships appeared off the English coasts. The king led the fleet that had brought him to England against them. His victorious men then needed payment, and the Londoners groaned as Canute exacted the sum of ten thousand five hundred pounds from them. This was followed by a tax on all the country for another seventy-two thousand pounds.

Canute then dismissed his fleet, sending all but forty ships to Denmark. He had disposed of all other claimants to his throne except Emma's young sons and Ironside's boys, the latter out of his reach in Hungary. He had won over the Church. There was no need for a standing army to intimidate his people. The time had come to present himself as a lawgiver, in the tradition of Saxon kings since Alfred.

An assembly at Oxford, where the greatest man after the king himself was Wulfstan, Archbishop of York, confirmed the laws by which Edgar had established peace and cooperation between the peoples of England. Under them, great men could not use the law for their own benefit and to the detriment of the poor. Archbishop Wulfstan, who understood law as well as theology, drafted the agreement, and he was to become one of Canute's chief advisers for matters both of Church and State.

In the year 1018, news came to Canute that distracted him from the consolidation of his position in England. His brother Harold had died, and Canute was heir to his kingdom of Denmark. It was necessary that he should cross the sea and show himself to his new subjects. Earl Thorkell was made regent during his absence in the North – which was to be the first of several.

The world of kings of England and Denmark – Havelok, Angys and Ogier the Dane – told as stories to little boys in days to come, was the inheritance of Hardecanute. It was his father's task to ensure this.

Since the death of Olaf Tryggvason, the rule of Norway had been divided between Earl Eric, Canute's friend, and the King of Denmark. Canute, now the Danish king, had no intention of breaking the connection with Norway, which had for so long been enriched by Viking raids and Ethelred's payments. Olaf Haraldsson, who had escorted Ethelred and Emma home from Normandy and may have fought with the Danes at London, had been proclaimed king over Thrandheim in the north-west. Norway for the Norsemen, said Olaf, and he was the most powerful man in the country.

Canute had a sister called Estrid who, with her husbands and children, moves in and out of the narratives of the late Viking Age. In the hall of Ulf, the Danish earl married to Estrid, Canute heard first hand of events in Denmark and Norway. But he felt the problem should be left to rest for the present, in the hope that Olaf's own men would overthrow him. So he returned to England.

Emma had the money, looks and taste that in the modern age would have inspired couturiers and designers to create for her transparent hats, high arched shoes, gowns of wild silk, collars of pearls or the setting of a single jewel in a velvet band. As it was, her role as restored queen was not to display herself before her people but to bestow gifts and patronage, above all on the Church. This she did to its entire satisfaction.

Out of the revenues which she had kept so carefully she bought and commissioned book manuscripts, written in Latin in the Caroline minuscule script named after the schools of Charlemagne where it was evolved. As if the text were not precious enough, the covers of the books were encrusted with gold, silver and gems.

Emma's brother Robert had been made Archbishop of Rouen, and she sent him a psalter. She and Canute also sent manuscripts to Germany and Scandinavia.

Richly embroidered robes and altar cloths worked in gold and silver – the threads carefully picked up with tweezers – and sometimes with the deep gold fringes known as orfrey, also passed from Emma's hands to churches. The wonderful medieval treasury at the Victoria and Albert Museum contains the kind of works of art with which she would have been familiar, although few actually date from her time. An exception is a crucifix known as a reliquary because it contained relics. It is made of beaten gold and cedarwood, with enamelled medallions and a realistic figure of Christ in sea ivory.

The approval of the clerics at the New Minster at Winchester was won with the gift of a tall golden cross enclosing relics. This was commemorated in the records of the New minster and Hyde Abbey, now in the British Library. A tinted drawing on vellum shows Canute wearing a crown too big for his head, cloak, tunic, sword and long socks, and Emma, robed and with a veil and tiara. The cross is between them.

Canute, who was credited with enough humility to realize he could not take his wealth into the next world, accompanied Emma further afield when he was available. They visited Sherborne in Dorset, where Wulfsin, a reforming bishop and follower of Dunstan, was buried in the unusually large and complex cathedral there. Shortly before his own martyrdom, Archbishop Alphege had arranged for Wulfsin's body to be moved into the cathedral, and miracles were reported at the tomb. But, as so often, valuables had been given up to pay tax and, as a result, the fabric of the building became neglected. Emma's quick eye saw gaps in the roof above Wulfsin's shrine. She gave twenty pounds of silver for its repair.

When land near Dorchester in Oxfordshire had been forfeited to Canute, he allowed Emma to give it to monks in Oxford. The king and queen particularly favoured the abbey of Ely and were granted special privileges there, along with Thorkell and Eric the Norseman. Emma gave cloths of silk and gold embroidered with jewels as well as a green-and-gold frontal for the high altar. This brought reminders of other times. Edward as a baby had been placed on the altar, and the abbey retained the shawl patterned with small green circles in which he had been wrapped.

Canute enjoyed listening to the singing of the monks as he was rowed to the isle in the Fens. None the less, his presence was a reminder of the time in the ninth century when Viking ships stole through the fens to kill and drive out the monks from Ely Monastery and set it on fire. It was one of the many painful associations he had to erase.

Emma ingratiated herself with the Church, but it does seem that she could have played her cards more skilfully in another direction. A hint to the churchmen that she would withhold her gifts unless they ordered Canute to banish Elgiva or, better still, marry her to a thane might well have had effect. Instead, while the queen presented her gifts, Elgiva embroidered altar cloths and persuaded Canute to give them to the abbey at Romsey. Worse still for Emma, it is likely that Elgiva was actually present on some of these royal visits.

The king held two great ceremonies, one to reassert his authority over the Saxons who had followed Ironside and the other to make amends for the slaying of Alphege, as he had long promised to do. He had ordered a church to be built at Ashingdon in Essex, the scene of his victory over Ironside, and went with the leading men of the Church, including Archbishop Wulfstan, for its consecration. Here Emma met the priest who was to become her chaplain in the years after Canute's death, and later Archbishop of Canterbury. His name was Stigand, and he was a curious, evasive, covetous character.

It was not until 1023 that Canute ordered that the body of

Alphege should be removed from St Paul's and taken to Canterbury. The clergymen and choristers, singing in praise of the martyr and the Lord for whom he had died, were joined at Rochester by Emma and Hardecanute, the stars of the show.

Although Emma collected and traded relics, she may have been a little chilled at the thought of having once seen the skeleton, now stretched out under its pall, standing fully fleshed and clothed, saying mass and giving out blessings.

The English people watched the procession across the Kent countryside and rejoiced to think that such scenes as the one at Greenwich were over. Their king had begun as a Viking but was now as true a Christian as any that had ruled over them.

At the end of the journey, Alphege was laid beside Dunstan in the cathedral at Canterbury. Emma presented rich gifts and Canute, in token of his kingship, gave a golden crown for the high altar. He also granted the port rights and privileges of Sandwich and some surrounding land to the monks of the cathedral.

The queen appeared to her people in her new incarnation, with the Danish heir at her side. But some remembered that Hardecanute and his sister, to whom Canute had given his family name of Gunhild, were not Emma's only children. The three she had borne King Ethelred lived across the sea because their step-father had no love for them.

Before this translation of Alphege's relics, a family event had taken place from which Emma had been entirely excluded. Canute's elder daughter, whose name is unknown, had been drowned in the millstream at Bosham. Her father buried her in the church, and he and Elgiva mourned her in private. Emma looked on, unable to intervene. At least she would make sure that Harold, Elgiva's son, would not claim blood relationship with her own children. Through her attendants she heard it was being said that Harold was the son of a cobbler and had been brought secretly to Elgiva's bed as a baby. She encouraged the circulation of this libel.

The year 1023 also marked the death of Archbishop Wulfstan and his burial at Ely. Wulfstan had said that a king is Christ's representative, who should protect his people and give them laws in accordance with the teachings of the Church. He listed the principles by which kings should live as being truth, patience, generosity, wisdom, dealing with wrong-doing, encouraging what is good, light taxation and rightful judgement. Canute's response to these exhortations was to codify secular laws, mostly governing property and based on the legislation of the Saxon kings, especially Edgar. The code was drawn up at Winchester one Christmas, when the men of the council had met to mix serious business with the festivities.

Thorkell the Dane, Earl of East Anglia and veteran of Ethelred's time, fell foul of the king and was outlawed. Canute was not showing any particular favours to Danes. However, when he went to Denmark again in 1023, he was not only reconciled to Thorkell but made him regent of the country and future guardian of Hardecanute, who was to be sent to Denmark. When Thorkell died less than three years later, Ulf, Canute's brother-in-law, was appointed regent and guardian in his place.

This Ulf, and his brother Eilaf, who had been given an English earldom, were men of false hearts. Ulf desired more than a mere regency. With Eilaf, Olaf Haraldsson of Norway and Anund, King of Sweden, he planned to raid Scania in the south, where much of Denmark's wealth was concentrated.

Canute had an intelligence network efficient enough to tell him of these plans well in advance and, having hastily assembled a fleet, he sailed north. Ulf, his brother-in-law, hearing of his coming, sent word that he submitted to him. But there were still the Swedes and Olaf's Norsemen to contend with.

In the Kattegat between Denmark and Sweden the Norsemen were met by the English ships and scattered. But Anund's fleet was waiting at the mouth of the Holy River in Sweden. Higher up the river was a dam built by Olaf, and the waters rose behind it.

Canute gave battle to the Swedes, but during the course of the fighting a roar of water was heard and a torrent poured out of the mouth of the river. It was the ships of Canute, rather than those of the Swedes, that were caught and swept away by the broken dam. The king escaped with his life, but the Battle of the Holy River was lost.

The Norsemen and Swedes did not pursue Canute, who was able to send a message to Olaf, offering to make him Earl of Norway if he would pay tribute to England. The offer was rejected. Canute retreated to Roskilde in Zealand, and Ulf accompanied him there. The king knew he had scotched the snake, not killed it.

He and Ulf quarrelled one evening over a game of chess, and the following morning Canute ordered one of his servants to kill Ulf. But the earl had gone to mass at St Lucius's Church, and the servant dared not touch him. Canute repeated the order to a more senior servant, and this time it was carried out. The assassin drove his sword through the earl in the church and when he left, his blade dripping with blood, the horrified monks locked the doors. Then Canute sent a command that the church should be opened again and mass resumed. Later he paid compensation in the form of a land grant. On his return home, Canute left agents to work against Olaf in Norway, spending much money to turn the people against him.

Olaf was a just king, a good administrator and a friend of the Church. He deserved the praise of his skalds, the poets of the North. During his reign, Norway, like Denmark and Sweden, continued to change from the land of hunters described by Ohthere to King Alfred into a country little different from the others of western Europe. Town life and trade increased. The great men in their halls had spices and Rhenish wine at their feasts, which were lit by beeswax candles. But the Norse king caused resentment by his severity in stamping out paganism, and many men were willing to take bribes and conspire against him.

It was about this time that Canute, knowing he was likely to be obliged to return to the North, made a South Saxon called Godwin the Earl of Wessex, the highest position in the country after the king, although much of Wessex consisted of royal estates. Godwin had been among the Englishmen who were loyal to Canute in the early years of his reign, accompanying him to Denmark when Olaf first fomented unrest. The two became friends and, to seal an alliance between English and Dane, Canute gave him Gytha, sister of Ulf, for his wife.

Godwin and Gytha had nine children, six sons and three daughters. At least one of the girls, Edith, was brought up in the abbey of Wilton near Salisbury. Tutors in the humanities, mathematics and arts and crafts were available here, and Edith became renowned for her learning and artistic talent. She spoke French, Irish and Danish, and her curriculum probably included grammar (study of literature) and music (the rules of plainsong and harmony).

The memory of Emma's older children was suddenly revived by news of the death of her brother Richard, the duke with whom Ethelred had made alliance. Messengers from his heir, Robert, gave assurance that he would gladly continue to give shelter to his Saxon cousins. This can only have been a relief, for Canute was by no means ready to entertain anyone who could be thought to have a claim to his throne.

In the town of Falaise in Normandy, the year after the Battle of Holy River, Duke Robert one day saw a French girl on the bank of the river, washing linen in the fast-running water. He paused to watch her and in that moment thoughts of the willing ladies of his court passed out of his mind.

Arlette, the daughter of the tanner of Falaise, became more to her lord than those others he had casually picked up, ravished and just as casually dropped. She remained in his castle, high overlooking the town, while Canute, concerned that the bonds of friendship with England would be loosened under Robert, offered him his sister Estrid, whom he had widowed by the murder of Ulf. The duke unwillingly accepted, but the marriage did not last and Arlette remained at the castle. Soon it was being said that Robert intended to make Arlette's son his heir. His name was William.

No matter how much Canute and Emma gave to the churches and abbeys of England, a pilgrimage was required for the Danish king to set the seal on his commitment to the Church. The Holy Land itself was held by the followers of Islam. But in Rome, the head of the Church, the successor of Peter, friend of Christ, extended a welcome to any who came with true reverence.

The time of the pilgrimage, breaking Canute's work in the North, was shrewdly chosen. As the first foreign King of England with overseas territories, he was mindful of the empire of Germany. Conrad II, who had been crowned with an iron crown in Lombardy, was to process further south to be crowned emperor with a golden one by the Pope. By attending the ceremony, Canute would both fulfil his duty to the Church and make alliances with the kings of Europe and the emperor.

His bishops reminded him that popes had always demanded exorbitant sums of money before they bestowed the pallium, a woollen cloak that was the badge of office, on the English arch-bishops. More urgent were the pleas of the leading merchants for the king's good offices in Rome on behalf of the traders crossing and recrossing Europe. Some sold rare and beautiful commodities for the glory of kings and the Church, others the timber, salt and grain that brought wealth to all the people.

Traders passed through the ports of the Low Countries and Rhineland and across the Alps into Italy, mostly by way of the Brenner Pass. Since the days of Charlemagne, one major route had run from Hedeby (now the town of Schleswig) on the Danish border, through Friesland on the North Sea to the Baltic and the rivers of Russia and on to the Caspian Sea and Persia. Besides the great rivers – Volga, Danube, Rhine – the merchants travelled along tracks that had been used by pack animals since the Bronze Age for the transport of drops of amber found on the Baltic coasts. The Vikings loved these, making them into jewellery or chessmen.

These journeys were arduous enough in themselves but, in addition, heavy tolls were levied at many points by the rulers of the lands through which the trade routes ran. The merchants' representatives begged Canute to win concessions in the atmosphere of goodwill generated by the coronation. They reminded him that pilgrims to Rome would also benefit.

Canute promised to do what he could and set out for Italy. The ceremony was to be held in March 1027, and much of the journey was undertaken in winter. Fortunately, the climate in the Viking Age was mild and warm, and spring flowers were seen in the months of snow and ice. The concept of foreign travel for enjoyment being unknown, Emma would hardly have thought she should accompany her husband – although she may have professed envy at the pious aspect of the undertaking.

Canute took many gifts, mostly relics and reliquaries, with him, and distributed them at the monasteries where he stayed on his way. At St Omer he was seen by a monk historian who was later to become well known to Emma. He reported that Canute made sure a reputation for piety ran before him by entering abbey churches followed by an attendant with a substantial gift for the abbey wrapped in his cloak. The king sighed and beat his breast, praying for mercy from heaven, and kissed the floor with tears. Then, at what he judged was the right moment, he gave a sign and the offering was given to him and placed on the high altar. Even the little altars in the side chapels received kisses and gifts. On emerging from the church, poor men waiting for him were also presented with gifts.

Once across the Alps, and steadily travelling beneath the high Italian sky, the party from England approached Rome. Like a plant whose fruits are carried far by wind, animals' coats and birds' wings, the ancient city had seeded many a field of England. Coins often, weapons and pottery sometimes, were turned up by ploughs in Wessex and Mercia. Floors of mosaic patterns and columns and busts of marble lay hidden in the earth, along with tableware of silver and gilt, decorated with figures of pipers and dancers to remind the diners of the youth and merriment of the pagan world.

Now the greater part of the city of Rome, following its sackings by Alaric the Goth and Gaiseric the Vandal, and the more recent destruction by the Saracen followers of Islam, resembled a rich garment thrown aside and left to moths and mice. A new community had sprung up on the ruins. Its people did not rule the city and *compagna* as the Caesars, consuls and senators had done before but attended the persons of the Pope and his inner circle and defended the city against further invaders. Some of these people were English, and a hospice for Saxon pilgrims had been founded by King Ine of Wessex on his visit in 720. King Ethelwulf had restored the hospice, which he had visited with his son Alfred. The English paid the Pope a yearly tax called 'Peter's Pence'.

Canute visited and made offerings at the churches built among the temples to the Roman gods. There were relics here in abundance. They were brought from the catacombs outside the city, where those who had known the Blessed Peter and Paul the Apostle had met in secret to take the meal of bread and wine that was the kernel of the inexpressible mystery of the mass.

The meeting of the former Viking with the Pope and the other Christian kings marked the official end of Northern paganism. The last feast had been held in Valhalla, and Asgard, city of the gods, was deserted. Nevertheless, their tales continued to be recited in the North for more than two centuries, for those people who found the Gospel stories a little tame in comparison. But it was the Christ, the Lamb of God, who now ruled over Europe, and kings and princes came with homage to his representative, the Pope.

Canute was given a hearing by both Pope John XIX and Emperor Conrad on the grievances of English pilgrims and merchants. Rudolf, King of Burgundy, who was present, also agreed to make concessions on road tolls. The Pope was willing to reduce the fees for the pallium.

The emperor in his turn had a favour to ask. He was seeking a wife for his son Henry, and his meeting with Canute convinced him that none could be more suitable than the daughter of the King of England. Through the mediation of the Archbishop of Hamburg the betrothal of Gunhild was proposed.

The promise of such a marriage for his little girl, together with his reception and the financial agreements, made the visit successful almost beyond Canute's wildest dreams. There was but one cloud on his horizon. The sons of Edmund Ironside were growing up with the status of royalty at the court of Hungary, and Canute felt they threatened the stability of his own kingdom. Conrad and the Pope could offer no help in the matter.

On the way home, Canute dictated letters to his people, to be read aloud in the shire courts. Besides recounting the concessions he had won for traders and pilgrims, he declared that he had vowed to rule well and put right whatever he had done wrong since becoming king – a safe promise, as murder and mutilation cannot be reversed.

There was work to be done in the borderland between England and Scotland when the king returned home. Lothian, the region from the Forth to the Tweed, became permanently part of Scotland, following the defeat of a Northumbrian army in 1018. But Canute led an army against Malcolm II, King of the Scots, who eventually acknowledged him as his overlord. The King of England also became Lord of Orkney and Shetland. Siward, the Danish Earl of Northumbria, maintained England's position as the dominant power on the border with Scotland.

Then the king turned his attention back to Norway, where the Norsemen had not yet risen against Olaf. Once Olaf was overcome and Norse nationalism suppressed, Canute would be virtually an emperor, ruling a great trading area which would bring prosperity to all his many peoples, the main source of that prosperity being England. It was a vision as glorious as the northern lights that rippled like many-coloured flames over Norway but as insubstantial as a crown of icicles.

He sailed with fifty ships from England, taking with him his heir, Hardecanute, then about ten years old. A Danish fleet joined them, but the ships looked in vain for signs of Olaf as they sailed along the awesome fiords of Norway, through emerald water and among blue whales like swimming islands. Local leaders were waiting for the King of England, and they gave him their allegiance when he came into their harbours. At last he reached Nidaros (now Trondheim), where the Norse kings received their people's homage, and was acknowledged as ruler.

Olaf fled Norway for Sweden, and Canute called the Norse earls and their followers together to witness his plans for both Norway and Denmark. Hardecanute was to be King of Denmark. Norway would be governed by Hakon, son of Earl Eric. But Canute, evidently uncertain as to how Hakon would deal with further nationalist rebellion, stayed in Norway until early in 1029.

On his return, the greatness of his achievements was set before Emma to console her for the absence of Hardecanute. Meanwhile, the sons of Elgiva continued to attend feasts, drinking deep in the company of the king and his men, even though their mother was a mere concubine in Emma's eyes. Her lot as mother of Canute's children was proving a hard one. Hardecanute, his father's heir, had been put under a heavy burden for one so young. And now Gunhild, her youngest, like her brother part of Canute's grand plan, was to be taken from her and would be made a bride while she was hardly more than a child.

At his feasts, the king summoned minstrels and poets to sing and chant of the battles of Brunanburh and Maldon, from the days when Saxon fought Viking and when they fell did so as heroes whose names were extolled throughout the land. Now the earls and thanes were content with their Danish king and had ceased to think of the line and sons of Ethelred, even in the presence of Emma, who had been his queen.

None the less, Canute, a conqueror and the representative of a race that had long wreaked havoc on the English, put a ring of steel between himself and his people. With him went a bodyguard of warriors, called housecarles and equivalent to thanes in rank. They were a brotherhood who stood close to the king in his halls and followed him to the battlefield. He also kept a fleet of Viking warships, originally forty in number, his own being a mighty vessel with more than a hundred oarsmen. The standing army and maintenance of the fleet were paid for by the English taxpayers, as was the dowry demanded for Gunhild's German marriage.

Canute had inherited the national currency established by Edgar and administered by leading men in the boroughs. With the help of these, called 'moneyers', he set up a similar system of mints in Denmark, where the first coinage had been of pennies like those struck in Ethelred's reign. Under Canute, Danish merchants in towns on the trade routes found silver pennies in plenty, and the country's prosperity increased accordingly.

In England, Canute's origins were acknowledged by adding a triangular helmet to the engraving of his head stamped on the coins. But England was quiet under the one-time Viking who had opened up new markets for his realm. Ships came safely to the ports, including London, with timber, herring, furs, flax, amber and pitch from the Baltic. This North Sea Empire extended as far as the Wendish tribes who lived between the Oder and Elbe rivers. The Germans had made a number of attempts to subdue the Slavic Wends and bring them to the Church, but they were still half pagan.

Now there came about something that pleased Emma greatly

and was also the strangest deed of Canute's reign. He required a governor for the Wends, who lived so far away, and appointed Sweyn, his son, with his mother Elgiva as his guardian.

For a woman to hold authority in such a land was startling enough, but for Canute to choose an Englishwoman, and the one he had held to in the face of the Church and his queen, is truly amazing. It seems that the hints of the churchmen that he should regulate his married life had at last prevailed. So Canute and Elgiva parted, and she went to Jomsburg on the Baltic, where the fiercest and most disciplined company of Vikings had recited their deeds of battle and voyages and rapine in verse, and took up the reins of government. A large company of Danes went with her and Sweyn.

In giving way to the Church, Canute granted Elgiva a higher authority than Emma, who had never been appointed regent during his absences. She had been allowed only to witness charters granting land. These were highly important legal documents, but signing them was not the equal of representing the king's person at home or abroad. If Emma and Elgiva had competed for political power as well as other favours of Canute, Elgiva seemed to have won, hands down. At least, though, her presence, reflecting Emma herself like an image in water, was gone. There would be no more watching the king turn his head at the sound of her footstep, no more seeing his eyes searching for her face among those around him, no more suspecting that he was sending gifts as tokens of a love she herself, although twice-crowned queen, had never had.

Earl Hakon, who had been set over Norway, came to England for his betrothal to a niece of the king. On his return his ship was caught in a storm in the Pentland Firth between Scotland and Orkney, and the earl was drowned. A messenger from Canute brought the news to Elgiva and Sweyn that he wished them to take up the much more important appointment of Governors of Norway. But during the lapse of time a man who was much nearer than the King of England acted swiftly.

Olaf Haraldsson, with Swedish troops, crossed the border into Norway and advanced on the Thrandheim region, whence Hakon had ruled and where Elgiva and Sweyn were awaited. He found, however, that Canute's agents had done their work too well. The Norsemen, instead of welcoming him, came against him at a place called Stiklestad, and there was a great battle in which the old warrior Olaf was slain.

Elgiva and Sweyn were greeted with enthusiasm on their arrival and established themselves as rulers in the royal hall. Elgiva had risen to a position that gave her authority over men who were still Vikings at heart. This needed careful and tactful handling.

She gave feasts and as hostess carried the mead cup to her guests, but when she sat with her son while he administered justice it became plain to the watchful Norsemen that it was the woman, not the youth, who was the governor of their land. They blamed her for the taxation and punishments for violence imposed on them and resented her train of Danes. Whereas, to most of the English, Danish and Norse Vikings were equally obnoxious, Elgiva in her loyalty to Canute showed a clear preference for Danes and their customs. The oath of one Dane in the law courts could over-rule those of ten Norsemen.

Anger spread through the land at the doings of this woman, not even the king's rightful wife, who would bring them under the heel of the Danes. But Canute held many Norse hostages, and it was known he would not hesitate to mutilate them or put them to death if reports of rebellion reached him.

Their regret for the rejection of King Olaf led a party to dis-inter his body, and churchmen pronounced the flesh sound as on the day of his death. He was taken to the church at Nidaros and buried in a state befitting a saint. Many people came to view the tomb, and reports of miracles began to circulate.

When Elgiva heard of them, she decided on a bold stroke and openly declared her disbelief in the incorrupt body. This heresy only made more people turn against her and, in late 1033, little more than three years after she and Sweyn had come to Nidaros, they found it best to leave for southern Norway, where feelings against them were less strong. The news when it was told to Emma gave her double satisfaction: the humiliation of her rival and the probable disqualification of Sweyn as King of Norway. Hardecanute, still in Denmark, was likely to inherit the whole of the North Sea Empire. Only his absence and the presence of Elgiva's son, Harold, at court spoiled her pleasure. This youth was renowned for his speed as a runner and men called him Harold Harefoot.

Far to the south in Normandy, Edward, Emma's eldest son, listened to the news from England as it was brought to him. Edward was happy in Normandy and had no wish to be reminded of England and his claim to its crown. He remembered only his schooldays at Ely with affection. Of his tribe of half-brothers, those who, like Edmund Ironside, had not met another *wyrd* had been slain by Canute. Edward had no intention of opposing such a man.

But the men of his family, including Count Dreux, married to his sister Goda, would not let the question rest. A crown is a crown, they said, and England was a prize beyond worth. Robert, Edward's cousin, was a believer in the near impossible. He even thought that his sturdy little bastard William, the tanner's grandson, would one day be Duke of Normandy after him.

Alfred, Edward's younger brother, less damaged by his mother's desertion, looked eagerly towards England, but Edward would far rather have remained in the company of monks and priests. He cared for no woman, least of all the mother who had chosen to wed the Viking and abandon her English children for him.

But Duke Robert kept up the pressure, and in the same year that Elgiva and Sweyn gave up trying to rule northern Norway Edward agreed to an attempt on England. It was a failure. After a storm, the fishermen of Jersey found Norman ships in their harbour and on board the impetuous Duke of Normandy and a timid man, white-haired although young. When the weather improved, the ships returned to Normandy and Edward to his quiet and pious life with its worship of Mary, the mother who had stood by her son on his cross and now reigned with him in heaven.

The invasion attempt was an embarrassment for Emma, but Canute set it against his relations with the rulers of continental Europe. The negotiations for Gunhild's marriage were well under way, and Emperor Conrad ceded territory on the Danish–German border to Canute. To advertise his country's wealth, the king regularly exchanged gifts with Emma's distant cousin, William, Duke of Aquitaine in south-west France, which was later to become a possession of England through its heiress, Eleanor.

Of his own Wendish subjects, one of their princes, with the outlandish name of Godescalc, joined Canute's housecarles. The friendship between them was such that the king gave him his great-niece Siritha in marriage.

By 1035 Canute was rising forty and Emma was in the region of fifty. If anyone had ventured to reckon on the length of a lifetime, Canute looked good for enough years to give his heirs maturity and experience. But late in the year his crown of icicles had melted and his imperial dream was over. Magnus, Olaf's son, was accepted as king throughout Norway. Sweyn fled to Denmark and Hardecanute, and Elgiva eventually returned to England.

Whether or not the loss of Norway through the woman he called his true wife broke his heart, the King of England was dead a few weeks later. The date was 12 November, the place Shaftesbury, sanctified by the burial of the young martyr King Edward. The final resting-place of Canute was the Old Minster of Winchester. Emma remained in the city after the funeral and with her the treasury of the kingdom.

EMMA THE QUEEN MOTHER

Throughout her life Emma had adapted herself. From her family in the small but stable ducal court of Normandy she had come to England to be its queen at a time of constant unrest and threats of invasion. After her Saxon husband died she had married the representative of the people who had terrorized him. With the help of the Church she and her Viking husband had been accepted by the leading men of the Saxons. She was a symbol of the good rule and prosperity Canute had brought to England.

During Ethelred's reign, except for the brief stay in Normandy, she had been surrounded by the rituals of queenship and the authority of the Church. Now, with Canute's unexpected demise, the first had been torn away. Her court was Godbegot, her home; her courtiers her retainers, Saxon, French and Breton. But she needed more than these to hold on to the treasury, the gold, silver, jewels and robes of silk and fur bought through trade and taxes by Canute. With them, and most significant, was the crown, the symbol of the kingdom due to her youngest son, Hardecanute, who had undertaken perilous voyages as a child, been thrust into power struggles in Viking lands and was now trying to keep the throne of Denmark against the Norsemen.

Harold Harefoot, son of her rival Elgiva, who hated Emma as much as she hated him, was in Wessex and would be king. From now on her life was to be governed by family events as dark and doom-laden as those of Greek tragedy.

If she had a thought of sending word to Normandy, it was dismissed. She did not know the exact standing of her other two sons there, and she was now a distant figure to them. Her nephew Robert had recently died while returning from pilgrimage to Jerusalem and with him Dreux of the Vexin, her daughter Goda's husband. The Norman lords and the King of France, Henry I, had half accepted William, Robert's bastard son, as duke; but no help could be forthcoming for Emma, his great-aunt. The boy was often under threat, but Arlette found ways of guarding her cub.

Once before, when King Edgar had died, two sons by different women had claimed the crown. Then Elfrida the Queen, who changed the course of the Saxon dynasty, had been obliged to give way but had later struck her blow for Ethelred. But she had had an accomplice, and the earls of Emma's day, if she had considered such a solution, would at least have hesitated. Earl Leofric of Chester and Mercia, who may have been related to Elgiva of Northampton, with the support of the crews of the king's fleet in London and the thanes north of the Thames, was for Harold Harefoot, as was Siward of Northumbria. Only Godwin of Wessex was willing to wait for Hardecanute to return.

For the first few days of her widowhood, it seemed that Harefoot might leave Emma and Gunhild to mourn undisturbed. Winchester regarded the queen as its own, and the chanting of the monks in the minsters and fall of the millstreams were sounds of comfort and reassurance. Then, suddenly, they were drowned by the clatter and shouts of troops in the streets. Harefoot's men had come to seize the treasury. They broke in, went through the locked boxes, took the greatest treasures, including the crown, and carried them away.

Because Harefoot's claim to the throne was disputed, Emma, unlike most widowed Saxon queens, was left in possession of her home and also of her lands and their revenues. When Harefoot's men had gone, it seemed that something could be salvaged after all. She stayed in Winchester awaiting the outcome of the council meeting to be held at Oxford to settle the succession – or her son's return, whichever came first.

It turned out to be the council meeting, and Leofric of Mercia put the case for compromise. Harold Harefoot, he said, should rule until Hardecanute came back to England. Earl Godwin demanded that Hardecanute should be proclaimed king and Harefoot excluded. The council combined the suggestions. Harefoot should be regent rather than king, while Godwin and Emma held Wessex on behalf of Hardecanute. It was also agreed that some of Canute's housecarles should attend on Emma.

This bestowal of partial political power was the best that could be done for the absent claimant and his mother. But it was an uneasily balanced situation, and how long it could last depended on how soon Hardecanute could return from Denmark. It was reported that Harold tried to force the issue by demanding that Ethelnoth, Archbishop of Canterbury, should crown him; but the archbishop laid both crown and sceptre on an altar, forbidding them to be removed, and Harefoot did not dare touch them.

The year drew on to summer with no sign of the rightful king. Instead, the envoys arrived to escort Gunhild to Germany for her marriage. The rich dowry had been paid and there must be no more delay. She was taken from her mother and, in due course, under the stately-sounding name of Kunigunde, was crowned queen of the great realm to which her husband Henry was heir.

In the same year Goda made a second, much less important marriage, to Eustace, Count of Boulogne.

Hardecanute and Magnus, son of Olaf Haraldsson and acknowledged King of Norway, continued to circle each other like two dogs. Back in England, Earl Godwin tested the currents of opinion as they moved now in the direction of Hardecanute, now, ever more strongly, towards Harold Harefoot. The sons of Ethelred did not enter into his calculations. He had heard that Edward was more like a monk than a prince and Alfred, although of different mettle, was younger and not the heir. Although they had the title of atheling (king's son), they were Normans rather than Saxons. It was to Saxons that Godwin looked for the fortunes of his sons, Sweyn, Harold, Tostig, Gyrth, Leofwin and Wulfnoth. There was also his daughter, the fair and learned Edith, waiting to have her future decided by her male relatives.

But now there was a new intervention on the part of one who had long stood in the background of Emma's life. Elgiva of Northampton had arrived in England, a widow but not a widow. The wealth she had acquired, whether in England or Norway, was being spent on buying legal confirmation of Harefoot's kingship. She made feasts for influential men, gave them gifts and asked for vows of loyalty to both herself and her son.

Canute was dead, but the memory of the old rivalry was revived. Emma's most dangerous enemy was the woman whom she had insulted, calling her a cheat in the matter of her son's birth. A man would have enemies of his own, but a woman stood apart from recognized hostilities and could, with cunning, use them to her advantage. And if Harold Harefoot was accepted by the council, Elgiva, not Emma, would be the queen mother. Godwin was cooling towards Emma's cause. One or other of the rightful king's half-brothers must come to her aid. Emma set about composing letters. They were sent to Hardecanute, asking him to return without delay, and to Edward and Alfred, lining them up as heirs to the throne if Hardecanute did not appear.

On the face of it, she was perfectly entitled to act like this. Although she backed Hardecanute and the House of Denmark, Emma had been forced to remember that Edward and Alfred were heirs to the House of Wessex. What she forgot was that they were now to all intents and purposes foreigners and their presence would not suit the plans and ambitions of the wealthy and ruthless men, notably Godwin, currently ruling the roost.

The letter to Normandy, from Emma, 'queen in name only', pointed out that by the death of 'our lord the king' her most dear sons were deprived of their kingdom. She enquired about their plans, as the usurper of their rule was constantly canvassing support from the country's leading men. These would prefer that Edward or Alfred should be king, so she begged that one of them would come privately to receive her advice as to how this should be brought about. She asked for an answer by return. She also wrote to Gunhild, feeling herself entitled to worry her newly married daughter with her difficulties.

Edward, reading the letter, was unmoved. He was to say later that his mother had always done less for him than he would have wished. The crown of England now belonged to the Danes, and Hardecanute, son of Emma's marriage to a Dane, would some time reappear and claim it. Harold Harefoot was but the son of a handfast marriage and said to be no friend of the Church. Edward would not leave Normandy. But Alfred, his younger brother, needed to win fame and fortune for himself. And he was eager to see his mother.

He sailed to Dover with a troop of Normans. The news of his coming was brought to Godbegot, where it set up a bustle of anticipation. It was also brought to Earl Godwin and the regent Harefoot.

The earl met Alfred and offered to escort him to Winchester and his mother. Alfred accepted what seemed to be an offer of friendship by the man more powerful than any in England except the one ruling as king. Godwin also swore to serve as Alfred's soldier. At Guildford Godwin made a feast for Alfred and his men and gave them accommodation in separate billets. In the night, a company of men sent by Harefoot attacked the camp. They took Alfred's men by surprise and executed them. Godwin arrested Alfred but did not keep him in his own custody.

Some time afterwards, the monks of Ely were disturbed at their prayers by shouts from a boat that had found its way through the Fens to their abbey. It carried Alfred, who, his face bloodied and ghastly, his eyes torn out, was given into their charge. The care of the monks and the medicines they applied to his injuries did little to relieve him, and in a few days he died. His maltreated body was buried with the honour due to his birth in the south side chapel of the abbey of Ely, which had been a place of happiness and safety for his brother Edward and their mother.

It was not with Emma but his sister Goda and her husband Eustace that Edward mourned Alfred and ordered masses to be said for his soul. But this was insufficient.

He was now willing to listen to those who told him he should become Saxon again and seek vengeance for his brother. He waited for the hour to come, along with his nephew Ralph, son of Goda. The Church, in the person of Edward's friend Robert, Abbot of Jumièges, attempted consolation and advised prudence. Edward also took a vow to make a pilgrimage to Rome, although it remained unfulfilled.

There was no king in England but Harold Harefoot, financing himself by such means as seizing the profits of Sandwich's herring fishery. One after another of the earls and thanes pledged themselves to him through Elgiva. She stood beside the king, now formally proclaimed, and was greeted as 'Lady'. This was enough. The struggle between her and Emma, as hard fought as any between Saxon and Dane, was won.

With the close of 1037 came the chance of the final humiliation of Emma. Word was sent to her that she could no longer remain in Winchester or indeed in England. She was to be exiled but in no danger of her life. It was not necessary to make a desperate flight across Europe as Edmund Ironside's widow and sons had done when Canute took the crown. Flanders, prosperous and stable, had links with the Saxons. A previous ruler, Count Baldwin II, had married Elfrida, daughter of King Alfred.

The Flemings, too, had had to fight for their survival against Vikings, but by the eleventh century they were at peace, with prosperity from the English wool trade. The present count, Baldwin V, had added more territory, including Antwerp.

The handsome elderly lady who came to his court at Bruges did not doubt her welcome. She was not only the widow of Canute but the mother of the Queen of Germany, the Countess of Boulogne and, of course, the King of Denmark and England; to say nothing of Edward, her eldest. Her devotion and generosity to the Church were widely known. She had brought enough money for her maintenance and even some for charity. Baldwin and his wife Adela granted her the refuge she required. She was but one of many, and the count did not always enquire closely into the claims some made on his hospitality.

Of Emma's stay in Flanders, while Harefoot and Elgiva dispensed justice and levied taxes on the English people, very little is known. She may have found the opportunity of a meeting with her French daughter Goda, whom she had not seen since she was a child. Certainly she would have known another little girl, Baldwin and Adela's daughter Matilda, who in due course was to be crowned Queen of England.

Emma had no escape from Alfred's murder. She received commiseration from her hosts, with the reminder that she had left him exiled in childhood. It was also known that he had come to England and his death in response to a letter from her.

Emma stayed two years in Flanders. In the year after her arrival, a cruel blow fell. Henry, the husband of Gunhild, the child closest to Emma, accompanied his father Conrad to Italy to quell a rebellion against the Germans. With him went his mother and Gunhild. On their return, disease broke out in their camp. Many died, and among them was Gunhild.

Magnus, King of Norway, agreed to meet Hardecanute to draw up a treaty between their two countries. Neither of them had an heir, and Hardecanute was unmarried. Indeed, the question of his marriage never seems to have arisen. The treaty proposed that Magnus should inherit Denmark in default of an heir to Hardecanute and Hardecanute take Norway if Magnus had no heir. Magnus believed he would be the one to benefit. Like his half-brother Harold, Hardecanute was often in poor health.

Hardecanute agreed to the arrangement. He was tired of the struggle to maintain his hold on his northern kingdom. Another richer southern realm awaited him. Its people would hail him as king and overthrow the usurper Harold Harefoot.

Nevertheless, because those people might almost have forgotten his existence after his long absence, he collected a fleet of sixty-two warships, which Magnus was willing enough to let him have, and departed in late 1039. His only legacy is the silver coinage of his reign. Under Hardecanute, they were struck with Canute's design of the head with a triangular helmet and the crosses and Lamb of God from Ethelred's time.

Hardecanute did not sail directly across the North Sea but along the coast of Flanders, where he left fifty-two of his ships in a harbour. He took the others to Bruges, arriving after a tempest. The appearance of a young man she would hardly have recognized seemed the fulfilment of Emma's hopes and longings. There had also been rumours from England that Harold Harefoot was ill and thought unlikely to live much longer. These were confirmed by the arrival of an embassy with the positive news that Harold had died in Oxford on 17 March. The crown was Hardecanute's for the taking.

Yet it was not until just before midsummer that he came to Sandwich with his full fleet and his no doubt impatient mother, to be hailed as king. He marked his accession to power by demanding a tax to pay for his ships' crews – thirty-two thousand one hundred and forty-seven pounds in all.

His thoughts now turned towards the sons of his mother's first marriage, Edward, living in Normandy, and Alfred, murdered so vilely. Hardecanute vowed he would take revenge for the murder, and Harold Harefoot, who had called himself his father's son, although dead, would not escape.

Hardecanute asked where Harefoot had been buried and was told that it was in Thorney Island by the Thames, where its tributary, the Tyburn, created a fenland. The king sent two of his officers, called Styr and Edric, on an errand of dread. They dragged Harold's body back into the sight of men and left it to lie in the marshes of the fen.

Between Westminster and Ludgate lived a colony of Danes, mostly married to Saxon women, who had their own church, dedicated to Clement, patron of sailors. A fisherman came to these people with the decomposing body of a man which he had found beside the river near the open grave of the late king. The priest of the Danes, believing it to be that of Harold Harefoot, carried it to the church and buried it there with honour.

Hardecanute accused Earl Godwin and the Bishop of Worcester of the murder of Alfred. The earl, being wealthy, was able to present the king with a warship and the service of eighty armed men, swearing that, in the matter of Alfred's blinding, he had only obeyed Harefoot's command. The king dared not disgrace him and instead sent to Normandy, asking his brother Edward to return.

Edward, seeing that the king would not avenge Alfred by overthrowing Godwin, agreed to go to England. With him went Goda's son Ralph and a number of high-born Normans and Frenchmen, to show that he came not as a Saxon exile but as the friend and relation of the young Duke of Normandy.

Despite the evidence to the contrary, Hardecanute possessed a streak of decency which showed itself in his dealings with Edward. He had, of course, no reason to feel jealousy over their mother. Receiving his half-brother with enthusiasm, he took him into his household and gave him a position of authority. They were an ill-assorted pair, the middle-aged, French-speaking man with Norman manners and tastes and the young, hard-drinking Dane, for whom his people had no love.

Neither of Canute's sons restored the glory of his times and his North Sea Empire. But, like his sister and half-brothers, Hardecanute might not live long. In that event, men said, it would be well to bring back the line of Ethelred, which was also that of Alfred and Edgar. They looked with favour on Edward the atheling who had returned home from Normandy.

Godwin continued to increase his power and promote the welfare of his family, but the two other great earls of England are remembered for other reasons.

In 1040, the year Hardecanute became king, a prince called Malcolm – afterwards Malcolm III of Scotland – came to Siward of Northumbria for protection after his father Duncan had been killed by the *mormaer* (ruler) of Moray and Ross, who had then seized the Scottish throne. The name of this man, who may have met Canute on his Scottish expedition, was Macbeth.

Leofric, Earl of Chester and Mercia, had married a wealthy and pious lady renowned for the length and thickness of her hair. The people of the little Midland town of Coventry, which had been sacked by Danes in 1016, came to this lady, whose name was Godiva, and begged her intercession with the earl for the heavy tax he had laid upon them. Perhaps Leofric, proud of Godiva's beauty, wished to display it before the eyes of his people. Or perhaps he remembered the pagan rite of a naked woman riding horseback and determined to give his town a double benefit. At all events, he promised to relieve the taxpayers if Godiva would ride naked through the market-place in Coventry and back again.

Godiva, with as much of her person hidden by her long hair as possible, set off on her horse. On her return, Leofric, a man of his word, called for a charter to be drawn up and the people of Coventry released from their taxes. Godiva then resumed her more conventional role as benefactress by gifts to abbeys in the west Midlands. She adorned a convent at Coventry which had been burned by Edric Streona with all the riches she could afford. But it is by her ride that she is known to this day.

Whatever Leofric's private arrangements, Hardecanute was still seeking collection of the tax for the crews of his warships. Two of his housecarles who had been given the task in Worcester were set upon by the men of the town and murdered where they had hidden themselves in the tower of the abbey. In return, the king sent more housecarles and militia to plunder and burn Worcester. He also allowed Edwulf, son of Earl Uhtred and Ethelred's daughter Elgiva, who was under his protection, to be murdered by Earl Siward. After this, Hardecanute was given the contemptuous title of 'pledge-breaker'.

With the same certainty as the cycle of the seasons, the monks appointed as chroniclers continued to record the times as they saw them. In the reign of Hardecanute they wrote of taxes and the price of eight bushels of wheat, of the disinterment of Harold Harefoot and the arrival of Edward, mentioning that he was the son of the Norman queen.

That queen, now back at Godbegot and established as mother of the king, without, for whatever reason, the presence of a young queen to take over from her, continued to witness charters, in which her name came after the king's. But the beneficent days of Canute were over, and later events preyed on her mind.

Emma would not have read the Old English of the chronicles, but she did understand the Latin of the Church. One of its practitioners had been a Welshman called Asser, who became a bishop, first of Exeter then of Sherborne. Few Britons achieved so much under the Saxons. He came to the notice of King Alfred and wrote an account of his life – no doubt the great king had his share of vanity.

It is just possible that Emma read, or had read to her, this Latin narrative. At all events, guilt over the murder of her son, resentment towards Elgiva and Harefoot, disappointment over Hardecanute and the perverse wish to proclaim her Danish sympathies moved her to make another career for herself within her queenship. Emma became a commissioning editor.

During her exile in Bruges she made acquaintance of a monk whose name is unknown, the same man who had commended Canute's religious excesses and whose monastery had benefited from him. His writing talents and flattery of Canute and Emma made him the ideal author of the encomium she had in mind. The research for this work and the first draft were carried out in Bruges. Emma occupied the editorial chair until she left for England, when the monk continued with the work according to her instructions. These included the statement – affidavit, almost – that it was Harefoot, not Emma, who ordered the fatal letter to be written and sent to Normandy, with the implication that Godwin was his accomplice in murder. Finally, there was to be no mention of her marriage to Ethelred.

The encomium, which is divided into three books, has been accepted as the main source of information for Emma's life. But it is a life that does not begin until, by the standards of the time, she was almost middle-aged. There is no child with her parents, no girl awaiting her betrothal, no young married woman. Instead the first book starts with Sweyn Forkbeard's antecedents and his decision to invade England. (Emma, of course, had not known Sweyn.) This is where the passages with the gilded and painted ships are found. The narrative moves quickly on to the conquest of England, the death of Sweyn and – Book II – Canute's return to Denmark when Ethelred was still king.

After the account of Canute's stay in Denmark, his relations there with his brother and Thorkell and the burial of Sweyn, comes the return to England, Edmund Ironside's resistance movement, the treachery of Edric Streona and the division of the English kingdom after the Battle of Ashingdon. It had been long since Ironside's death, and Emma agreed that it should be ascribed to the wish of God himself that England be reunited. With Ironside in his royal tomb, Canute took possession of his English kingdom. Now Emma herself appears at this cut-off point in her life, when she was free of Ethelred and separated from his children. To account for Canute's willingness to marry her, she is described as the most fitting bride who could be found for him, a paragon of nobility and wealth, beauty and wisdom.

Then Hardecanute was born and baptized, and other sons (whose paternity is blurred) are brought up in Normandy. The ghost writer flatters him as much as he does his mother. As for Canute, he lived like a bishop and a monk, built churches and generally devoted himself to pleasing God. In the secular world he cared for widows and orphans, practised justice and kept his people in peace and unity. His death ends Book II.

In reality, of course, Emma had been steadily finding it more difficult to deal with three factors: the presence of Elgiva, the hostility of her son Harold Harefoot and the fact that Hardecanute was in Denmark. The writer occasionally refers to Elgiva as 'some other woman' or 'a concubine' and to Harold as a serving maid's son. But in Book III he is obliged to come closer to the truth, although he calls the letter to Normandy a forgery. In response came the landing of Alfred the atheling in England, his meeting with Godwin, the execution of his men at Guildford and his blinding and death through Harefoot's agents.

The flight of Emma to Bruges is related, then the arrival of Hardecanute, his joyful reception by his mother, the messengers from England and his return with Emma. After Hardecanute's acceptance as king, he summons Edward from Normandy and the two rule with their mother, united in love.

The encomium is the story of the Danes who ruled England and the queen who guided the present Danish king safely to his rightful inheritance. Emma evidently understood the concept of what is now called 'reinvention'; she might also be called a mistress of self-deception. Certainly the one thing the encomium does not show is her heart.

When finalized, the text, written and decorated on vellum by two scribes in north-east France, was garnished with display capitals and coloured letters. A presentation copy, now in the British Library, is introduced by a picture of Emma enthroned, accepting the book from its writer, with her sons Hardecanute and Edward looking on.

Every book is aimed at a readership. Emma's, her surviving sons, was small, although she may have visualized descendants of Hardecanute reading it and saluting her memory. It may be safely assumed that Edward gave particular attention to the details of his brother Alfred's murder.

In the year 1042 the chroniclers recorded that calamity came upon England, with the failure of harvests and disease of cattle throughout the land.

More of the king's business was being transacted in London, and, on the eighth day of June, Hardecanute the King rode to the wedding feast of one of his father's retainers, known as Tovi the Proud. It was held at the royal manor of Lambeth, across the river from Thorney Island, where Hardecanute had ordered the desecration of the body of Harold, his father's son. The feast was flowing with drink. The guests applauded as the king, the first guest, came into the hall. He was given a drinking cup or horn and set it to his lips.

As the guests cheered and the bride and groom looked on, the king's face became distorted and purple with swollen blood vessels and he fell upon the floor in convulsions. In a few minutes he had gone to join Havelok, Angys and Ogier, kings of the united land of England and Denmark, and his own father Canute, who had ruled an imperial realm that, to modern eyes, seems hardly less legendary.

EDWARD THE KING AND EDITH THE QUEEN

Before Hardecanute had been buried in the Old Minster at Winchester, every man of influence in London declared that Edward should be king. The people of the city, hearing how Hardecanute had met his *wyrd* at Lambeth, added their voices of approval. The rule of the Danes was over.

Edward was visiting Normandy, where Duke William was eager for him to take the English crown. Edward was reminded yet again that the murder of his brother was unavenged. To leave Normandy for good was painful, but Abbot Robert of Jumièges was willing to accompany him. As King of England the appointments to English bishoprics would be in his hand. There was much he could do both for his friend and for the Church.

The trouble caused by the delay of Hardecanute in claiming the crown showed that a king should have an heir close at hand. The sons of Edward's elder brother, Ironside, were still in Hungary. It perhaps did not enter his mind that the same argument would be applied to himself and, his brother being dead, he would be expected to marry, which he had no inclination to do.

In due course he presented himself at Gillingham in Kent, where a meeting of the council was to be held confirming his election as king. Godwin assured him of his wholehearted support. He seemed unaware that anything was unresolved between them.

And Edward, listening to him, unwillingly recognized that, if he wished to rule England successfully, the earl, with his wealth, power and cunning, was the best ally he could have.

Edward's way of life had not including money-making, so some of Godwin's resources went to making the vote for him certain, even though it meant that England and Denmark would no longer be joint kingdoms. After it had been cast he was enthroned in Christ Church, Canterbury, where Emma had been married for the first time and crowned queen. He then set out for Winchester.

Emma, still in residence at Godbegot, had no reason to think her position as queen mother would be altered by Edward's accession nor that she need amend her lifelong attitude to him. Hardecanute had been her favourite; why pretend otherwise now he was dead? She was as well established in her position as any royal woman could be, thanks to her care of the money from her estates. She had a number of faithful retainers, including her chaplain Stigand, whom she had first met with Canute at Ashingdon. Although he had been chaplain to Harold Harefoot, she felt he was a man whom she could trust.

In the North, Magnus of Norway had invaded Denmark and was insisting that his agreement with Hardecanute made him King of England, too. Nevertheless, he sent messages of friendship to Edward, as did the rulers of Germany and France. Henry III of Germany, who had been the husband of Edward's half-sister Gunhild and was now married to Agnes of Poitou, sent ambassadors with presents and sought to make alliance with him.

There was general astonishment at the turn of events but optimism as well. Canute's line had rotted away, and the only person who would not admit it was his widow, Emma. It began to be whispered that she would like to see Magnus as king and England returned to the Viking line.

Edward was crowned in the Old Minster on Easter Day, 3 April 1043. The crown contained a rare and beautiful stone brought from the East, blue as a cornflower and clear as spring water. It was to become known as St Edward's sapphire.

Edsige, Archbishop of Canterbury, reminded Edward at some length of his responsibility towards the English who were now his people. They may have had a Saxon king again but one whose heart was Norman.

The reign started badly. Edward had to deal with the problem of food shortages as well as learning the English ways of government. He was busy – but not too busy to listen to what was being said of his mother. Emma was reported to have sent to Magnus with an offer of her own money to finance his invasion of England.

On the face of it, this accusation was absurd. Magnus was a Norseman not a Dane, and Emma of all people knew the difference. By far the most likely explanation is that she had been garrulous, indiscreet and over-confident in her hold over Edward, the reluctant king. Perhaps she was a little unhinged with misfortune. No doubt she had enemies, and their gossip did the rest.

Unfortunately, Edward saw no reason to make allowances for her. In the reign of his father Ethelred she had allowed her servant to open the gates of Exeter to Sweyn Forkbeard. She had shared the bed of Forkbeard's son Canute and his concubine. Her partiality for the Danes had infected the Saxon court, causing treacheries to break out like so many boils. And she, not Harefoot, had written the letter that had lured her son Alfred to his unspeakable death in England.

At Gloucester Edward called together his triumvirate – Earls Godwin, Leofric and Siward – without whom he could make no important decisions. He told them of his suspicions of his mother, adding, 'She has been very hard on the king, her son.' All the self-pity of his deserted childhood is in that phrase.

The earls advised him to move against Emma and her chaplain and counsellor Stigand and would accompany him to see the fun. In November, the four set out on the ride to Winchester. Having gained entry to her home, it is unlikely that Edward directly referred to her marriage to Canute. Instead, he charged her with inviting Magnus of Norway to claim the English crown and offering him her gold and silver for the venture. For such treason, against both the king and the land of England, she was to lose her moneys and her lands. Stigand, her friend, would be deprived of his possessions and his bishopric of Elmham in East Anglia.

Emma defended herself as well as she could. But the time had long passed when she could have made up for the carelessness that had brought about the wild accusation. She had chosen to follow the fortunes of the conqueror, and he and their son were now dead. Edward, Ethelred's son, was king and for some unaccountable reason wished to be rid of her.

She remained in Winchester because there was nowhere else for her to go, and in time placatory messages were brought to her. The king would allow her enough income for her needs, but she was to stay in retirement for the rest of her life. Underlying the command was the desire that she should enter the Church, but, despite her displays of piety, she would not do this. One thing remained to her and she would keep it: her home, Godbegot.

For the remaining nine years of her life Emma was an onlooker, only occasionally appearing at court or receiving visitors: the shamefaced king, perhaps her daughter Goda, who had ordered the building of a church at Lambeth, or her grandson Ralph, who was to leave the only line of Emma's descendants, as Gunhild's daughter Beatrice entered a nunnery. She heard of the doings of the king and the earls and of events overseas, especially in Normandy.

The young William, now a knight, was successfully imposing his authority on his rebellious barons, some of whom were related to him, sometimes in opposition to Henry, King of France, some-times with his aid. Then a great victory, the battle of Val-ès-Dunes in 1047, made him master of all Normandy, including the Channel coast from where he could launch a fleet against England any time he chose. Men said that William had the qualities of a great general and trembled in his presence. Yet he was also devoted to the Church and was without the lechery, intemperance and extravagance that had brought others down.

It was a strange *wyrd* that had given a tanner's daughter such a son while a twice-crowned queen had borne a drunken fool and one who prayed to God while listening to libels against his own mother. But the event that moved Emma most was the marriage of the king, and this finally displaced her on the chessboard of England.

To be fair to Edward, few would have seen anything unusual in his removing his mother when he took a wife. There was not room at court for both the king's mother and the queen. The difference was the accusation he brought against Emma in the presence of the three great earls, well before he was compelled to take a wife.

For the third reign in succession England had an unmarried king, and Edward made a virtue of the chastity of his life. He believed it dated from his dedication at Ely. Such a king had never been known before, and the churchmen declared he was a blessing to the land. But he was now not far off forty years old, without an heir, and necessity decreed he should marry.

Canute and Ethelred before him had been unwilling to obey the demand but not out of sexual disgust. Edward had, however, already learned that the king must listen to his council. Especially Earl Godwin.

If Alfred had died, like Hamlet's father, 'unhouseled, disappointed, unaneled' and his ghost had walked and urged vengeance for his murder, Edward might have nerved himself to accuse and arrest the earl, always affable, always protesting his loyalty. But the tomb was silent and the king had learned to control his horror of Godwin, the smoking gun, who had given him a warship and crew. Inevitably, when he asked the name of the bride his councillors had in mind, it was that of Edith, Godwin's daughter.

The Godwins had caused praise of Edith's beauty and learning to be circulated while they kept her in the nunnery at Wilton and argued over her future. She was now some twenty-five years old. Edward knew that an English bride, even one who could speak French, would please those who were murmuring against his Norman followers. He gave way and went back to the pre-Ethelred custom of choosing a queen from a powerful English family. On 23 January 1045, the king placed his thin hand with its long fingers in that of Edith and swore himself to her in marriage. She was consecrated as queen, probably at Winchester.

Now comes the question of whether the marriage was consummated. William of Malmesbury, the later but authoritative chronicler, passed on gossip that it was not. There is no reason to think this was untrue. The stability of the state largely depended on full sexual congress between a king and queen, and there would have been eyes and ears stationed behind wall hangings to make sure it took place.

So Edith, released from Wilton, where she was never wholly one of the community because her father and brothers were keeping her available for their idea of a great marriage, now found herself at the centre of national events but still chaste as a nun. No doubt she confided the situation to her mother but probably not her mother-in-law. She and Emma met in London in the year of her marriage, a formal occasion when both the young and the old queen witnessed a charter.

Earl Godwin and his sons could now come freely into Edward's presence. If they reproached him with his sexless marriage, by which no heir of their house could be born for England, the king quietened them by pointing to the many estates he had bestowed on Edith. Edward himself was the greatest landowner in the country, but Edith held land throughout Wessex, from Devon to Berkshire and Kent, also in Essex and Suffolk, and in the Mercian counties of Gloucestershire, Buckinghamshire, Rutland, Northamptonshire, Lincolnshire and the nunnery and manor of Leominster on the border with Wales, as well as houses in towns, including Bath, Sherborne, Canterbury and Worcester. England had recovered well from the stripping of its assets by Ethelred and the Danes, and Edith's revenues made her even more wealthy than Emma had been.

Edward had no experience of war, but in the summer of 1045 the rumours from Norway obliged him to go to Sandwich and command thirty-five ships there. No invasion came, but old men and women told tales of the days of the Viking raids, and the name of Magnus roused almost as much fear as that of Sweyn Forkbeard.

By the end of the following year he had taken Denmark from the other claimant, Sweyn, son of Canute's sister Estrid, who asked England for fifty ships. This request was refused and Sweyn fled, leaving Magnus as unopposed King of Denmark. The terror in England increased, and throughout 1047 watchmen on the headlands daily expected to see the Norseman's sails approaching. Then, suddenly, news was brought that banished that fear. Magnus had died in October, and the Norse threat appeared to be over at last.

The reality of land, to those who lived and worked on it rather than merely receiving its revenues, was recorded in the 'Domesday' survey of 1086, thirty-four years after Emma's death. It was commissioned at Winchester, where the returns from the hundreds, filed under the names of tenants, were kept. (Scribes at this time were much in demand, for the writing of the national chronicles continued, with the comment that every hide and yard of land and every farm animal was recorded by the Domesday clerks.)

Such detail helped to enforce the payment of land tax and other dues to the king, including those for his sport. The survey dealt not only with early Norman England but also with the reign of Edward the Confessor, whose estates were called the ancient demesne of the Crown. Much land was in the hands of the Church, dating from the tenth-century Reformation. The value of its estates is also recorded, and it was high.

Winchester itself was left out of the survey, as was London, but revenues in Hampshire, for example, were raised from riverside meadows where grass was cut for hay, from water mills, with the eels in their pools, from fisheries and salt pans on the coast. Timber and charcoal came from forests such as Sherwood, Wyre and the Kent and Sussex Weald, which covered large stretches of England. Vines were cultivated, a reminder of the prevailing mild climate. The Domesday Book shows rural England regulated and quiet, in between outbreaks of disease. Edward's reign can to some extent be compared with the years when his grandfather Edgar, called the Peaceful, was king. This was partly because of the retreat of the Vikings to their own lands and in part to Edward's personality. There was also the influence of Edith, who helped him to cultivate a kingly image.

She had accommodated to her marriage and the empty cradle by the employment of her needlework skills. The rich garments the king wore at festivals and the gold-embroidered cloths for his throne were made by the queen, who also provided miniature birds and animals in gold for his horse's trappings. Edward himself commissioned Sparrowhawk, Abbot of Abingdon, a goldsmith, to make a new crown for him.

But after Canute, whose courtiers laid on the flattery while shaking in their shoes, Edward's presence was like mild evening air.

He had, inevitably, some eccentricities. One was a habit of suddenly bursting into loud laughter at table, whereupon his disconcerted companions fell silent. The other oddity was his attitude to money.

For some reason he was one day in his treasury, but hidden, when a thief broke the padlock of a chest of coin. Edward watched him until he heard his treasurer, Hugolin, approaching, then cried, 'Make haste! If Hugolin finds you, he will not leave you a single coin.' The thief ran away, and Edward told the treasurer the story. 'Enough is left,' said the king. 'The thief needed it more than either of us and should keep it.'

But this was nothing compared with Edward's failure to grasp the rise of English nationalism after the end of Danish rule, and his lack of appreciation of Saxon culture, even with its tradition of learned and artistic churchmen. In the previous century, Archbishop Dunstan had been a scholar with a knowledge of Latin and Greek, an instrumentalist and composer of music and so skilled in metalwork that he is called the patron saint of goldsmiths. Elfric, Abbot of Eynsham in Oxfordshire, who was educated at Winchester, was a brilliant teacher who raised the standard of written English, translated the Old Testament from Latin and recorded much of the life of the countryside in his own time.

If he could have spent his days with men such as these, Edward would in all probability have come to respect the English and been willing to learn their language. But the manners and outlook of the earls and thanes around him, led by the terrible Earl of Wessex, filled him with resentment and contempt. He let it be known that his court was open to Normans, Bretons and Flemings who wished to make their fortunes in England. Churchmen from Europe who came for funds were given a sympathetic hearing, and even promoted within the English Church. The king shut his eyes to simony, the offence of buying or selling preferment in the Church.

Perhaps because his mother lived in Winchester, Edward seems to have spent much time in London. In 1044 he appointed Abbot Robert of Jumièges to its bishopric. He had spoken to Robert, his closest friend, of his plans to build a great abbey church in the Norman style in London. Robert had brought the ill feeling against Godwin into the open by sending the earl a message to the effect that he should have no peace from the king until he restored his brother to him – in other words, never.

Edward could find no escape from his in-laws, who went from bad to worse. Sweyn, the eldest son, who had been given an earldom, carried off the abbess of the nunnery at Leominster owned by his sister, Queen Edith. Forbidden to marry the abbess, he escaped to Denmark, where he committed another serious crime and was sent back to England with eight ships.

A number of ships had been sent from Edward's fleet at Sandwich to beat off raiders from Ireland who had landed in the south-west. On one of these, waiting at Pevensey in Sussex for a wind, was Beorn – nephew of Godwin's Danish wife, Gytha – who had also been given an English earldom. Edward seems to have wished to reconcile Earl Godwin to his attitude to Edith by ennobling even his remote relations.

Sweyn reached Beorn's ship and asked him to come with him to Sandwich and mediate on his behalf with the king. They found horses and set out, but by some argument Sweyn persuaded Beorn to go with him to Bosham instead. Here Sweyn's men kidnapped Beorn and murdered him on board ship.

The king was still waiting at Sandwich. He assembled his army and told them of Sweyn's crime. The verdict was that he should be outlawed and named *nithing*, or without honour. To deal with a man who had violated all rules of decency and right doing, King Edward turned to the Vikings for what was judged to be the most appropriate and effective punishment. Only the ever hospitable Baldwin of Flanders was willing to give shelter to Sweyn Godwinson afterwards.

After this episode, Edward laid off his standing fleet and, a little later, he abolished the tax that provided for both housecarles and warships. The people of England were at last given a break from taxation, but their south coast was left largely undefended.

Edward had chosen the site of a new palace complex with the great church dedicated to St Peter, the building of which freed him from his broken vow to go on pilgrimage to Rome. On Thorney Isle in the fenlands of the Thames were the remains of St Peter's Church founded by King Sebert of the East Saxons in the seventh century. Dunstan brought the first monks to a later abbey, called the West Minster. Edward's new abbey was to prove his greatest legacy and full justification for his decision to take the crown. Being away from the port and from the ancient City of London, Westminster became an area of significance in its own right, at first for Church and later for Parliament.

Edward's friend Robert was to be Archbishop of Canterbury, and he undertook the journey to Rome as part of his appointment. Edward had found the courage to reject Godwin's candidate, but in the same year, 1051, he was drawn into the wrong side of a quarrel with the earl.

Count Eustace, the husband of Edward's sister Goda and an ally of Duke William, came on a visit to the king and probably also called on Emma. On his return, Eustace and his men stopped in Canterbury for a meal, then set out for Dover, which lay in Godwin's earldom of Wessex. Wearing his coat of mail, the count, speaking as the king's guest, demanded the best lodgings in Dover for himself and his men. One of these chose a particular house but was turned away by its owner. The Frenchman wounded the man of Kent and was killed in return. Eustace mounted his horse, rode to the house and killed the man. The affray spread quickly. About twenty men were killed on each side, and the whole town was roused against the French. Eustace called together his remaining men and rode away across the country until they reached Gloucester, where the king was staying.

Edward listened to Eustace's version of the story and flew into one of his occasional rages on his brother-in-law's behalf. The punishment for the civil disturbance, which had been used in similar circumstances by his predecessors – even Edgar – was clear. Edward called on Godwin and ordered him to go to Dover and wreck homes and workshops there. Godwin refused to take such action against his people. Archbishop Robert, hearing the refusal, which amounted to treason, cried to Edward that now was the time to overthrow the man who had murdered his brother.

Godwin withdrew from the king's presence, and with his sons, Sweyn (who had been given another earldom) and Harold, called together the militia of their earldoms and, at the beginning of September 1051, brought them to the Cotswolds, near the king's country residence. Edward, terrified, sent for Leofric and Siward, who hated Godwin. They appeared with their own militia. Ralph, the king's nephew, also came with troops.

Edward now had an army strong enough to defy Godwin, but the consequences of such a battle alarmed him and his councillors. Godwin, too, was uneasy about fighting the king, who was also his son-in-law. It was therefore agreed that the armies should give hostages instead and the Godwins present themselves before a meeting of the council in London to answer the king's case against them. Instead, Edward used his authority as king to call out all the militia of England, including the Godwin followers. Having taken away their powers of rebellion, and after attempts to bargain by Godwin, Edward ordered him and his sons to go into exile within five days.

Godwin and his wife Gytha and three of their sons went to Sussex, where a ship was waiting for them in Bosham creek. They loaded it with treasure and set out for the court of Count Baldwin. Harold and his brother Leofwin went to Bristol and found their way through much bad weather to Ireland.

Only Edith, Godwin's daughter and Edward's queen, remained, but Archbishop Robert persuaded the king to complete the break by sending her back to the nunnery of Wilton. Now all the Godwins, not merely Edith, seemed caught in a vacuum. Soon after midsummer, however, news came that Godwin had landed at Dungeness in Kent, where he obtained enough promises of help to see that many men would support him against the king.

Bad weather kept Edward's ships away and they were brought to London to be overhauled. But this took a long time, and, soon after Godwin had returned to Flanders, the crews of the English fleet in the Thames abandoned their ships.

Godwin sailed back to the south coast, which he plundered for provisions, and met Harold with a fleet west of Portland. They went along the coast, collecting seamen and ships from the ports of Kent and Sussex, and eventually came to London, which they knew to be on their side.

The size of his opponents' fleet as it surrounded his own much smaller one and the mediation of Emma's chaplain Stigand, now Bishop of Winchester, made Edward go revert the original arrangement. After Godwin had appeared before the council to defend himself, Edward's policy was reversed. Godwin and his sons were given back all their possessions and privileges, and any lingering hope of vengeance for Alfred was extinguished. The Frenchmen in England were outlawed if their loyalty was in doubt. Stigand was made Archbishop of Canterbury in Robert's place.

Edith, of course, was included in the armistice. She left Wilton and, with whatever willingness on the part of the king, was restored to her place in his bed and at his board.
But, by this time, autumn 1052, Emma, the queen mother, was dead.

*

If she was eighteen at the time of her marriage to Ethelred, Emma lived to sixty-eight, a great age for that time. Imagination has to be called upon to recount her thoughts and memories and the details of her daily life. Those who wrote *The Anglo-Saxon Chronicles* had lost interest in her, the 'Old Lady, called Emma', the chess queen who had been taken off the board and put into the box.

Of course she was not alone. She had her servants, for whom she had made provision, and one or more of them would have accompanied her when she watched the procession of the pilgrims to St Swithun's shrine or walked among the market stalls and by the millstream that was the boundary of the estate left by King Alfred to his wife Ealhswith. To the nuns of what used to be called the Little Monastery, rebuilt in stone by the reforming Bishop Ethelwold, Emma would have seemed hardly more substantial than the ghost of their patron, Ealhswith. They and all others in the city would have greeted her kindly, but she was a reminder of an age that had gone, an age that had melted like the snows of yesteryear.

Life was not an empire under the northern star, nor even the brotherhood of kings and popes in Europe. Emma's best days had been when Hardecanute and Gunhild were small children and she herself rode with Canute to churches and abbeys to distribute precious and beautiful gifts. But the land had never been her own, despite her two crownings. It is likely that her memory extended further still, beyond even her marriage to Ethelred, and that the last land in her mind was Normandy.

It is not known if Emma died quietly or at the end of a long illness, nor what sins she confessed to her priest, nor whether she was consoled by a vision of her younger son, healed of his grievous wounds. The date was 6 March 1052. It was a landmark that was soon swallowed up as the country moved into uncertain times under its childless king.

Edward buried Emma with Canute. His sister Goda died not long after. The date of the death of Elgiva of Northampton, who had shadowed Emma so persistently, is unknown.

It may have been in the same spring that William of Normandy, with many French retainers, came to England to call on the king. And Edward, divided between guilt, thankfulness and perhaps real sorrow that now he must wait until heaven for all to be put right between himself and his mother, resolved that William should rule England after he himself had been laid to rest in his abbey at Westminster.

AFTER EMMA: FROM SAXON TO NORMAN

During the last thirteen years of his reign, Edward's reputation for sanctity increased, and he was regarded as the kind of saint called a confessor, having resisted worldly temptations without being martyred. He originated the custom in England of touching people to cure the 'king's evil', a form of tuberculosis called scrofula. Until the eighteenth century many continued to believe that the monarch had the power to heal this disease.

In the secular world, the office of chancellor dates back to the reign of the Confessor, and he brought in the Norman practice by which a reigning king or queen seals instead of signs documents. Each king has his own seal, usually with the design of a crowned figure on a throne. King John did not sign Magna Carta; he attached his seal to it.

Earl Godwin survived his restoration for less than a year. While dining with the king in Winchester at Easter, he was laid low with a stroke and died a few days later. The earldom of Wessex passed to Harold, his eldest living son, who became as dominant as his father had been. He warred against a Welshman, Gruffydd, who called himself 'King of all Wales' and entered into alliance with Elfgar, son of Leofric of Mercia and Godiva. In 1058, Gruffydd and Elfgar joined with Norsemen from Norway and Viking settlers from Dublin, the Hebrides and Orkney against England. The

English chroniclers say little about this, but the invasion attempt was a major one.

Gruffydd married Aldgyth, Elfgar's daughter. Her mother was the daughter, by her first marriage, of Edward Ironside's wife of the same name. Elfgar and Harold continued the rivalry of their fathers, Leofric and Godwin, but, after Elfgar died in 1062, Harold and his brother Tostig pursued the Welsh king until Gruffydd's own men murdered him in Wales, cut off his head and presented it with the figurehead of his ship to Harold. The trophies were brought to Edward, who can hardly have regarded them as other than deeply barbaric. Wales was ravaged in the Viking tradition, and for generations footprints were seen across the land in the form of stones inscribed 'Here Harold was victorious'.

Harold then married Aldgyth, Gruffydd's widow, despite a longstanding handfast marriage to another Edith whom, like Canute with Elgiva, Harold did not cast aside.

Meanwhile, Queen Edith retained her position. She and Edward had reached a compromise in their marriage under which both busied themselves with religious foundations – he at Westminster, she at Wilton, where she had the church rebuilt and consecrated with much ceremony. Edith also witnessed many charters and had a say in church appointments.

Like Emma before her, Edith commissioned a Flemish monk to compose an encomium, not of herself but of Edward, and it was written just after the Norman Conquest. It seems that her memories of her unfulfilled marriage and of other instances of Edward's behaviour had softened considerably. In the *Life of King Edward Who Rests at Westminster*, his marriage is presented as the only possible one for a king who was also a saint. It was by the evil counsels of Archbishop Robert, according to Edith, that Edward took her estates and her gold and silver and sent her back to the nunnery at Wilton.

Outwardly, Edith was as successful a queen as Emma, although she and her brother Tostig were suspected of involvement in the murder of a Northumbrian thane, Cospatric, son of the Earl Uhtred of Ethelred's reign. But the question of an heir to England loomed ever larger as Edward grew older. Magnus of Norway had been succeeded by Harald Hardrada, his uncle. Both he and Sweyn of Denmark, son of Canute's sister Estrid, were known to be eyeing England up.

Although his own reign had effectively ruled out the claims of Edmund Ironside's descendants, and despite his likely pledge to William of Normandy, Edward sent the Bishop of Worcester to negotiate with Emperor Henry III for the return to England of Ironside's son Edward. This meant the young Edward giving up a royal career in Hungary, where he had married Agatha – perhaps a daughter of King Stephen – and when he eventually came back to England in 1057 he died before meeting the king. Another possible claimant, Goda's son Ralph, died the same year.

Westminster was consecrated on 28 December 1065. On 5 January, Emma's eldest and only surviving child was on his deathbed, attended by Edith. The following day, he was buried at Westminster, and there, the same day, Harold Godwinson was crowned king. This is the only time that the brother of a Queen of England has subsequently become King of England.

William prepared to make good his claim to England, while

Harald Hardrada, King of Norway, quoted the treaty his nephew Magnus had made with Hardecanute, promising each other their kingdoms in default of direct heirs.

Harold II ruled from London, and it was here that news was brought that a fleet under Harald Hardrada had appeared in the Yorkshire Ouse. The Mercians and Northumbrians fought a battle at Fulford, near York, but after great losses the leading men of York were forced to make peace with the Norsemen. Hardrada and his army waited for the northward-marching Saxons at Stamford Bridge, a crossing of the river Derwent. King Harold took them by surprise on 25 September, and after a hard fight Hardrada was killed and his army scattered. With this decisive battle the Viking Age of England was finally at an end.

Throughout the summer, William, Arlette's son, had been planning the invasion of England. It would follow the Norman victories in southern Italy and Sicily. As well as Normandy, men and ships came to him from Brittany, Aquitaine, central France, Flanders and Italy. Among the leaders was Count Eustace of Boulogne, Emma's one-time son-in-law.

Henry IV of Germany promised help if William needed it. The Church, now weakened by the separation of the Orthodox Church of Constantinople twelve years before, made its presence felt. Pope Alexander II gave the enterprise his blessing, on the prompting of a much greater man, Hildebrand, later Pope Gregory VII.

A favourable wind brought William with his armed men and horses to Pevensey on the Sussex coast. Harold led his tired and depleted army on the long march through England and engaged the invaders in what is now known as the Battle of Hastings on 14 October. There Harold met his *wyrd*. His housecarles failed to save him – among the mêlée of mail-clad cavalry depicted on the Bayeux Tapestry – and by nightfall he was slain.

The Saxon defeat, said the monk writing his chronicle at Worcester, was because of the sins of the people. He was mistaken. It was because William's army included cavalry and the Saxon one did not, and William's leadership qualities and personal charisma were greater than Harold's, renowned warrior though he was.

Aldgyth, whose life shows parallels with that of her namesake and grandmother, was in London during the Battle of Hastings. Afterwards, her brothers took her to Chester for safety, and there she vanishes from history, a shadowy, tragic figure, king's wife but not queen, in whom the chroniclers lost interest in the excitements of the new rule.

This time there was no stand by a valiant warrior, true heir to the throne, and a countrywide rally against the conqueror. Only Edgar the atheling, grandson of Ironside, was in Wessex, and the Saxons proclaimed him king.

William and his army left Hastings after five days and marched to Canterbury and on to Winchester. Edith, still of royal status although among a conquered people, was in residence there. The Normans negotiated with her in French, and she accommodated herself to her latest difficult situation. She handed over the keys to Winchester and capitulation followed, Edith being left free.

William continued his advance, but rather than storming London directly he led his army in raids through the surrounding countryside. Before long, Edgar gave up his meaningless title of king, and his men in London accepted that Emma's people were in England for good. Their leaders, with Saxon earls and bishops and Edgar the atheling, acknowledged William as their lord at Berkhamsted in the Chilterns.

On Christmas Day 1066, just under a year after Edward's burial there, William was crowned in his abbey at Westminster. But it was not until the spring of 1068 that his wife Matilda, daughter of Baldwin of Flanders, came to England and by her coronation at Westminster finally displaced Edith as queen. Being descended from Alfred the Great, she brought Saxon blood back to the royal line. Like Emma, she was to be the mother of two kings of England: William II, called Rufus (1087–1100), who was killed while hunting in the New Forest, and Henry I (1100–35), born in England, the wisest and most just of the Norman kings.

Edgar gave up the unequal struggle and with his mother and sisters, Margaret and Christina, escaped to the royal court at Perth and the protection of Malcolm of the Scots. This was the king who killed Macbeth.

Yet there were some who believed that these warriors from France, more efficient and better organized than the Vikings had been, might yet retreat to their own coasts and Saxon, Briton and Danish settler be ruled again by the House of Wessex. Two years after the Conquest, the south-west rebelled against the Normans. Edith's mother Gytha, a formidable Danish lady bereft of her sons by Hastings, was a rallying point, but she was forced to flee, along with a number of Saxon noblewomen. For a while they stayed on Flatholme, a little island in the Bristol Channel, and eventually they reached Flanders.

Harold had defeated Norway, but Denmark still had an interest in England. In 1069, Danish ships appeared in the Humber and were followed next year by King Sweyn. His presence moved the local English to rebel. Led by a Lincolnshire thane called Hereward, they occupied Ely and with Danish help sacked Peterborough Abbey before its Norman abbot arrived there. However, William and Sweyn came to an agreement that the Danes should withdraw. This left Hereward and his men to continue their defiance, with the support of the Abbot of Ely, and they were joined by Morcar, Aldgyth's brother, who had been Earl of Northumbria.

William laid siege to Ely, but Hereward made a daring escape through the Fens. No one knows when he died, but he was like an earlier Robin Hood to both Normans and Saxons.

Edith would have heard reports of the fearful 'harrying of the north' carried out by William in 1069–70, something that gentle King Edward would never have dreamed of. As well as the arrival of the Danish fleet, there was a revolt in Mercia, led by Edric, nephew of Edric Streona, allied with princes of the Welsh Marches. Edric had never acknowledged William's authority. But the king defeated him and passed with his chariots of wrath to York to finish off the Danes there. After they withdrew, William burned and plundered the countryside, starving the people of Yorkshire and the north and west Midlands into submission. No one in Mercia and Northumbria was left in doubt as to who was king in England, and most of the remaining Danes were wiped out.

Men lost in the mountainous country of west Shropshire have claimed to see a huntsman swooping with howls and shrieks over the ridge called the Stiperstones. It is said to be the ghost of Edric, called the Wild, riding on the memories of his terrible times.

It was in 1070 that the Scots King Malcolm III married the Saxon Princess Margaret, later St Margaret of Scotland. Their daughter Edith became the wife of Henry I and was known as Matilda. This marriage restored the line of Ethelred, although not through Emma, and it has continued unbroken to this day. Elizabeth II, having given her third son the Saxon name of Edward, revived the title of Earl of Wessex for him.

Despite his military might, William also wished to be accepted as the rightful heir of his cousin Edward, Emma's son, and therefore saw that respect was paid to his widow. He had taken enough from the Saxons who fell at Hastings to leave Edith in possession of the lands Edward had given her. She felt sufficiently secure to visit abbeys and ask for treasure as though she were still queen. At Abingdon, this treasure included priestly robes and a copy of the Gospels adorned with jewels and gold.

She continued to live at Winchester and Wilton, and the last mention of her is as witness to a charter in 1072, when she was described as 'the Lady'. She died in her fifties on 19 December 1075. Her body was brought from Winchester by command of King William and buried near Edward in Westminster.

Thus Edith, despite her Danish blood, takes her place in the history of England as a Saxon, while Emma, who began as Norman, became first Saxon, then Viking and was finally reclaimed in death by the Normans.

FAMILY TREE FOR EMMA'S FIRST (ENGLISH) MARRIAGE

= marriage or equivalent

House of Wessex
871 (Alfred)–1066 (Edward the Confessor)

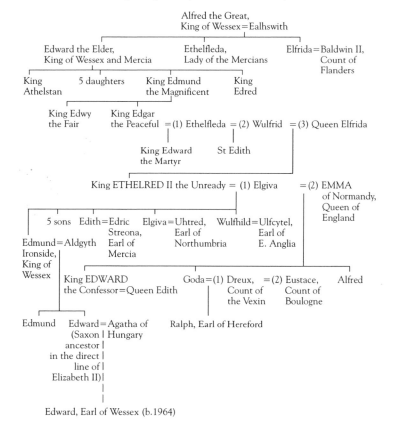

FAMILY TREE FOR EMMA'S SECOND (DANISH) MARRIAGE AND QUEEN EDITH

= marriage or equivalent

House of Denmark
1014 (Sweyn I Forkbeard)–1042 (Hardecanute)

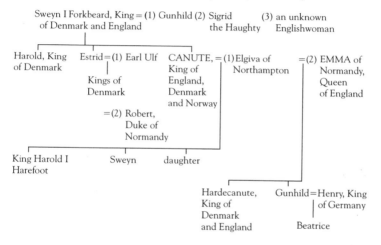

Sweyn I Forkbeard, King = (1) Gunhild (2) Sigrid (3) an unknown
of Denmark and England the Haughty Englishwoman

Harold, King of Denmark

Estrid = (1) Earl Ulf
Kings of Denmark
= (2) Robert, Duke of Normandy

CANUTE, = (1) Elgiva of Northampton
King of England, Denmark and Norway
= (2) EMMA of Normandy, Queen of England

King Harold I Harefoot

Sweyn

daughter

Hardecanute, King of Denmark and England

Gunhild = Henry, King of Germany

Beatrice

House of Godwin
January–October 1066 (Harold II)

Godwin, Earl of Wessex = Gytha (sister of Earl Ulf)

King Harold II = Aldgyth

5 sons

Queen EDITH = King EDWARD the Confessor

DATES OF THE PRINCIPAL EVENTS
OF EMMA'S LIFE

984   Emma born in Normandy (possibly Rouen)

1002   Emma's marriage to Ethelred II and her coronation;
St Brice's Day Massacre (13 November)

1003   Sweyn Forkbeard invades England; birth of Emma's
son Edward

1004   Raids and sackings in East Anglia

1005   Severe famine; Danes leave England; Alphege made
Archbishop of Canterbury

1006–7   Danes return and devastate countryside until paid
off; birth of Emma's daughter Goda

1009–12   More Danish invasions, culminating in murder of
Alphege

1013   Birth of Emma's son Alfred; Sweyn and Canute sail
to England and Sweyn proclaimed king

1014   Emma and Ethelred and their children refugees in
Normandy; death of Sweyn; Ethelred, accompanied
by Emma, returns at his council's request; Canute
leaves England

1015   Rebellion of Edmund Ironside against his father
Ethelred; return of Canute

1016 Death of Ethelred; series of campaigns by Ironside ends with Danish victory at Ashingdon; meeting between Canute and Ironside; kingdom divided, Ironside king only of Wessex; death of Edmund Ironside; Canute becomes King of all England

1017 Marriage and coronation of Emma and Canute

1018 Canute inherits Denmark from his brother Harold

1019 Birth of Emma's son Hardecanute

1023 Reburial of Archbishop Alphege in Canterbury

1027 Canute attends coronation of the German emperor in Rome, arranges betrothal of Gunhild, his and Emma's daughter, to the emperor's son Henry

1030 Canute's handfast wife Elgiva and their son Sweyn made Governors of Norway after the death of Olaf Haraldsson, King of Norway

1035 Death of Canute; Hardecanute in Denmark; Elgiva's son Harold seizes the king's treasures left in Emma's charge at Winchester

1036 Council appoints Harold regent of England while Earl Godwin and Emma hold Wessex for Hardecanute; Gunhild leaves for her German marriage; Goda marries Eustace, Count of Boulogne; Elgiva returns to England, raises support for Harold; Emma writes to Normandy for help; her son Alfred comes to England, is ambushed by Harold and Godwin and dies after being blinded

1037 Harold proclaimed king; Emma ordered into exile, takes refuge in Flanders

1038 Death of Gunhild; writing of the encomium begun

1039 Hardecanute comes to Flanders, takes Emma with him to England

1040 Death of Harold; Hardecanute made King of England, rules unjustly

1042 Death of Hardecanute; Edward comes to England, proclaimed king

1043 Edward accuses Emma of supporting the claim of Magnus of Norway to the English throne, orders her into retirement; she spends the rest of her life in Winchester

1045 Marriage of Edward to Godwin's daughter Edith

1052 Death of Emma in Winchester

APPENDIX 2

REMAINS AND MEMORIALS

The Normans wrote their character in stone on the face of England as they brought in new and more effective methods of warfare, defence and punishment. Their castles, which began as wooden buildings on earth mounds, developed into great stone keeps with dungeons in which those being punished were condemned to living deaths. Many of these structures have now fallen into ruin, but the White Tower of the Tower of London dates from the reigns of William the Conqueror and Rufus. William I confirmed London as England's urban centre, although he and his sons continued to keep the Treasury at Winchester.

When Emma came to England in 1002, less than 10 per cent of the population lived in towns. Nevertheless, urban living was on the increase and had taken a great leap forward because towns could be fortified against Viking invaders. The science of town planning evolved rapidly.

But in scores of cities and towns in England it is as though the Saxon and Viking settlements, their homes with thatched roofs and wooden walls, their markets, craftsmen's shops, churches and cemeteries, have simply vanished. Although the chronicles of this time are as full of humanity as the woodland is of birds, it has taken much dedicated work by archaeologists to find the artefacts used by ordinary people – as opposed to manuscripts, which were guarded like treasures – and map the streets where they lived.

In Winchester, it is not until after descending the High Street to Abbey House on the site of Ealhswith's foundation and the towering statue of Alfred that the Saxon city is brought to mind – unless a detour is taken to view the artefacts in the City Museum. The cathedral is, of course, Norman. Bishop Walkelin, who succeeded Emma's friend Stigand, was given the task of demolishing the Old Minster – disturbing the royal burial ground in so doing – and raising a much larger cathedral. He ordered stone from the Isle of Wight and oak timber for building materials. More work was done in later centuries, but the Norman transepts remain today, their Romanesque columns and rounded arches showing how a warrior people could yet construct the first steps of the ladder to heaven.

Pilgrims continued to attend Swithun's shrine for the healing properties of his relics, crawling close to them through a tunnel under a platform. His bones were scattered during the Dissolution of the Monasteries.

Bones that may be those of Emma, Canute and other kings, relics of a different kind, were collected and stored, eventually reaching the mortuary chests now seen on the presbytery screens. Research on dating and identification is, at the time of writing, being carried out by the authority on Winchester Cathedral's history, John Crook, who has supplied photographs for this book.

Dr Crook believes there is a real possibility that the bones of Emma and Canute are indeed in one or more of the chests, but Winchester has not done well by them or Edith in its official publications or in the museum. However, the Museums Service can give details of Emma's home, which disappeared after the twelfth century. It was described in the survey called the 'Winton Domesday' carried out in the reigns of Edward the Confessor and Henry I. Emma left most of the tenement to the Church, and this was confirmed by Edward. Later, various people, including the reeve of Winchester but not the king, had rights in it. Two market stalls paid twopence a week to Emma's chapel. A small notice on the wall of the present-day building refers to the derivation of the name but makes no mention of Emma herself.

Elsewhere in England, principally in London and Wessex, sites associated with other characters in this narrative are indicated by a few lines that briefly bring them and their times to mind.

Plaques at both Southampton and Bosham claim to mark the place where Canute is said to have rebuked his courtiers' flattery by ordering the waves to retreat, but the so-called Canute's palace in Southampton dates from the twelfth century.

At Holy Trinity Church, Bosham, a place where one steps straight back into pre-Conquest England, a Victorian vicar excavated the tomb of the nameless little girl, Canute and Elgiva's daughter. A stone coffin from Canute's time with some small bones was found, and a tile with the design of a raven near the chancel arch of the church now marks the grave.

At a second excavation in 1954, another Saxon coffin, complete with a man's skeleton, was discovered. It has been suggested that this was either Earl Godwin or King Harold, but neither is likely (permission to exhume and investigate the bones further has been denied, so we may never know). Godwin's grave is believed to be at Winchester, and Harold's is probably at Waltham Abbey in Essex, which he founded. Another abbey, at Battle in East Sussex, was built by William, its altar marking the spot where Harold fell.

The Goodwin Sands off the east Kent coast were once a stretch of low-lying land belonging to Earl Godwin. They were protected by a sea wall which was later allowed to crumble and let in the sea.

A few English churches are dedicated to Olaf Haraldsson, in his post-warrior career as St Olaf of Norway. One of these is St Olave (Hart Street) in the south-east of the City of London; another, in Chichester, is now a bookshop.

Paintings of Godiva and her ride, executed by artists from 1586 onwards, are on exhibition in the Herbert Museum and Art Gallery, Coventry, and her statue is near the Cathedral Lanes shopping centre.

Hardecanute's death is mentioned in the guide book to the Museum of Garden History, formerly the church of St Mary-at-Lambeth, next to Lambeth Palace on the south bank of the Thames. The guide also gives details of the fatal wedding feast and the date of 1062 for Edward's donation of Lambeth to Goda. The distinguished translator of Emma's encomium, Alistair Campbell, says that Goda died soon after 1051.

The church of St Clement Danes in the Strand was rebuilt after its destruction in the Second World War, and its rededication as the Church of the Royal Air Force has wiped out all trace or mention of Harold Harefoot.

A restored Hawksmoor church, the parish church of St Alfege

in Greenwich, stands on the site of the murder of the Archbishop of Canterbury, whose name is more usually spelled Alphege. A tablet to his memory declares that 'He who dies for justice dies for Christ'. He appears in two modern stained-glass windows in the church – the originals were destroyed in bombing during the Second World War. Alphege's story is told in round windows in Canterbury Cathedral, where he can also be seen on a Victorian altar frontal.

The relics of Ethelred's brother, King Edward the Martyr, were disinterred from Shaftesbury Abbey in 1931. They were eventually given to the Brotherhood of St Edward, of the Russian Orthodox Church in exile, and since 1988 have been kept in the monks' chapel at Brookwood, the Surrey necropolis beside the line to Waterloo. Rather puzzlingly, it was decided that the Orthodox, not Catholic, doctrine would have been familiar to Edward. Corfe, where he was murdered, has a church dedicated to him.

A fifteenth-century brass memorial set in Purbeck marble indicates the burial of Ethelred I, King Alfred's brother, in Wimborne Minster, Dorset. When Emma and Canute visited the tomb of Wulfsin at Sherborne, they may also have seen the tombs of two more of Alfred's brothers, Ethelbald (who married his stepmother, Judith) and Ethelbert, both briefly kings. Two stone coffins in the abbey, one of which is still visible, are said to contain their bones.

There is no overlooking the Confessor's memorial, although his name, like that of William the Conqueror at the Tower of London, is almost lost among so many others from English history. Edward was made a saint in 1161. Saints have attributes by which they are recognized, and Edward's was a ring. It was said that he gave this to a beggar, who was actually the writer of St John's Gospel in disguise. A few years later, two pilgrims on the way to Jerusalem met St John, again dressed as a beggar. He gave them Edward's ring and told them the king would be with him in heaven in six months' time – which duly occurred. Edward's chapel was largely rebuilt by Henry III in the thirteenth century, a task that involved moving Edward's remains. A shrine of gold and jewels was plundered during the Dissolution, and Edward's relics, along with the legendary ring, disappeared. Around the chapel lie later kings and queens, tidied away in their tombs. If a quiet moment can be found among the tourist hubbub, this is a fitting place to meditate on the workings of *wyrd* as expressed in the seventeenth century by James Shirley:

> The glories of our blood and state
> Are shadows, not substantial things;
> There is no armour against fate;
> Death lays his icy hand on kings.

The rose-cut sapphire in the Imperial State Crown, dating from Queen Victoria's time, is believed to be taken from the crown used at Edward the Confessor's coronation. This crown is worn at the State Opening of Parliament. The one that has been used for coronations since Charles II's reign has inherited the name of St Edward's Crown from the original monarch's crown. Edith's somewhat tawdry crown – silver gilt, decorated with coloured stones and glass – was worn by kings' wives until the reign of Charles I.

Contemporary likenesses of Saxon and Danish kings exist but are usually unsatisfactory as the art of portraiture had not been mastered. All the kings appear on their coins as faint outlines on tiny, worn pieces in museum cases. Edward and Edith are both to be found on the Bayeux Tapestry in France. The British Library cares for manuscript paintings of Edgar and Canute, the latter being shared with Emma. She also has her encomium frontispiece (shown in the plate section of this book), in which she is accompanied by Edward and Hardecanute.

Reverence for Edward, once patron saint of England, lingered through the centuries, and he is one of the saints accompanying Richard II in the London National Gallery's sublime late fourteenth-century Wilton diptych. His place in the line of English kings is acknowledged in various cathedrals throughout England, including an image in the medieval east window in York Minster.

The pictures of Emma in the British Library are not portraits but representations of royalty. But is the final verdict on Emma to be based solely on her status? Is she an historical curiosity? An ivory queen, finally pushed off the chessboard of England by kings, queens, bishops and knights of her own stock? A political figure who attempted to swim against the tides of a thousand years ago? Or a wife and mother trying to operate in a context of murder and treachery?

The question is still being discussed by scholars. The jury is still out.

SOURCES

TEXTS

Britannica CD2000, britannica.co.uk

Brown, Michelle P., *A Guide to Western Historical Scripts from Antiquity to 1600*, London: British Library Publishing, 1993

Campbell, Alistair (ed.), *Encomium Emmae Reginae*, Camden Third Series, Vol. LXXII, London: Offices of the Royal Historical Society, 1949

Campbell, James (ed.), *The Anglo-Saxons*, Harmondsworth: Penguin Books, 1991

Churchill, Winston S., *A History of the English-Speaking Peoples*, Vol. I, London: Cassell and Co. Ltd, 1956

Clark, John (ed.), *Alfred the Great: London's Forgotten King*, London: Museum of London, 1999

Clarke, John, *An Introduction to Brookwood Cemetery*, Brookwood Cemetery, Surrey: Necropolis Publications, 1992

Crook, John, *Winchester Cathedral*, Andover, Hampshire: Pitkin Unichrome Ltd, 1998

Dales, Douglas, *Dunstan: Saint and Statesman*, Cambridge: Lutterworth Press, 1988

Davidson, H.R. Ellis, *Gods and Myths of Northern Europe*, Harmondsworth: Penguin Books, 1964

Doubleday, H. Arthur (ed.), *Hampshire and the Isle of Wight*, Vol. I,

The Victoria History of the Counties of England, London: University of London Institute of Historical Research (reprinted from 1900 edition by Dawsons of Pall Mall, London), 1973

Encyclopaedia Britannica, Chicago, London and Toronto: Encyclopaedia Britannica, 1957

Fletcher, Anne (based on an original text by David L. Edwards), *Lambeth Palace: Official Souvenir Guide*, London: Lambeth Palace, 2000

Gibb, J.H.P., *Sherborne Abbey*, Sherborne Abbey, Dorset: Friends of Sherborne Abbey, 2000

Holmes, George (ed.), *The Oxford History of Medieval Europe*, Oxford: Oxford University Press, 1992

Kilpatrick, Betty (ed.), *Brewer's Concise Dictionary of Phrase and Fable*, Oxford: Helicon Publishing, 1993

MacDonald, Jennifer, *A Millennium Tale of Monarchs, Murder, Mystery and Mayhem*, Trowbridge: Wiltshire County Council, 2000

Marwood, G.W., *Holy Trinity Church, Bosham*, Chichester, West Sussex: Selsey Press, 1995

Montague-Smith, Patrick W. (original text), *The Royal Line of Succession: The British Monarchy from Egbert AD 802 to Queen Elizabeth II*, Andover, Hampshire: Pitkin Unichrome, 1999

Postan, M.M. and Edward Miller (eds), *The Cambridge Economic History of Europe*, Vol. II, Cambridge: Cambridge University Press, 1987

Reuter, Timothy (ed.), *The New Cambridge Medieval History*, Vol. III, Cambridge: Cambridge University Press, 1999

Richards, Julian D., *Viking Age England*, Stroud, Gloucestershire, Tempus Publishing, 2000

Roesdahl, Else, James Graham-Campbell, Patricia Connor and Kenneth Pearson (eds), *The Vikings in England and in Their Danish Homeland*, London: The Anglo-Danish Viking Project, 1981

Rutherford, Lucy, *St Alphege*, Bath: Friends of Bath Abbey, 1997

Salzman, L.F. (ed.), *Cambridge and the Isle of Ely*, Vol. I., *The Victoria History of the Counties of England*, London: University of London Institute of Historical Research (reprinted from 1938 edition by Dawsons of Pall Mall, London), 1967

Stafford, Pauline, *Queen Emma and Queen Edith: Queenship and Women's Power in Eleventh-Century England*, Oxford: Blackwell, 1997

Staniland, Kay, *Embroiderers*, London: British Museum Press, 1994

Stenton, Sir Frank, *Anglo-Saxon England*, Oxford History of England Series, Oxford: Oxford University Press, 1943

Stephen, Leslie (ed.), *Dictionary of National Biography*, London: Smith Elder and Co., 1886

Swanton, Michael (ed.), *The Anglo-Saxon Chronicles*, London: Phoenix Press, 2000

Whitelock, Dorothy, *The Beginnings of English Society*, The Pelican History of England Vol. 2, Harmondsworth: Penguin Books, 1981

Whitney J.P. (ed.), *The Cambridge Medieval History*, Vol. III, Cambridge: Cambridge University Press, 1930

Wilmot-Buxton, E.M., *Britain Long Ago*, London: Harrap and Co., 1906

Winchester Museums Service, *Nunnaminster: A Saxon and Medieval Community of Nuns*, Winchester, Hampshire: Winchester City Council, 1993

Winchester Museums Service, *Saxon Winchester Official Guide*, Winchester: Winchester City Council, 1995

MUSEUMS

Ashmolean Museum, Oxford

British Library, London

British Museum, London

Herbert Art Gallery and Museum, Coventry

Kingston-upon-Thames Museum

Museum of London

Museum of Oxford

Orkney Museum, Kirkwall

Salisbury and South Wiltshire Museum

Winchester City Museum

Yorkshire Museum, York

INDEX